Adventures in Camping

An Introduction to
Adirondack Backpacking

Adventures in Camping

An Introduction to
Adirondack Backpacking

Barbara McMartin

with Lee M. Brenning

Illustrations by Scott D. Selden

NORTH COUNTRY BOOKS, INC.
Utica, New York

Published by North Country Books, Inc., Utica, New York, 13501

Copyright 1996 by Barbara McMartin

Library of Congress Cataloging-in-Publication Data

McMartin, Barbara.
    Adventures in camping : a young people's guide to Adiron-
dack backpacking / Barbara McMartin with Lee M. Brenning :
illustrations by Scott D. Selden.
      p. cm.
    ISBN 0-925168-54-8 (alk. paper)
    1. Camping—New York (State)—Adirondack Park—
Guidebooks. 2. Backpacking—New York (State)—Adirondack Park— Guidebooks. 3. Adirondack Park
(N.Y.)—Guidebooks. I. Brenning, Lee M., 1955- . II. Title.
GV191.42.N7M32   1996
796.54'097475—dc20   96-15000
                                  CIP

For the grandchildren, who already love to go camping

Ali, Casey, Lisa, and Dan

With thanks to Betsy Folwell for editing this book and making many important suggestions. Thanks also to my sons-in-law--Dick Loomis for his artistic advice and Bob Lawrence for helping the children enjoy camping. Lee M. Brenning, my coauthor on so much of the Discover the Adirondacks *series, helped with a quarter of the trail descriptions, and his help is always much appreciated. Scott Selden's sketches depict the pleasure my grandchildren have had in learning how to camp. They also illustrate effectively the many things campers need to know. And, special thanks to my grandchildren for their patience in being models for the sketches.*

Contents

Let's go camping

Let's go backpacking

Let's go camping. Let's go backpacking. You can walk farther into the forest, explore remote places you can barely reach on a day hike, and best of all, you can be close to the natural world. You can find lakes for swimming, places to pick berries, ponds for fishing. You get to sleep out at a campsite so far from lights and settlements that you can see more stars on a dark night than you have ever seen before. If you are lucky, the northern lights may blaze across the sky. You can puzzle over the funny names of the places you visit--Grizzle Ocean, Queer Lake, or Puffer Pond. Was Hour Pond really an hour's walk from Old Farm Clearing? You can wonder about the first people to visit these distant places--who were the Johns or Streeters or Sargents whose names are remembered in the lakes you visit? You will be in places so remote that you can imagine you are one of the first explorers. Even if you do not see moose at Moose Pond, you may see bears, beavers, or otters and maybe even a fisher. Best of all, you can gain a sense of independence in learning how to be self-reliant and responsible in new, wild places.

Before you go camping you may want to read *Adventures in Hiking, A Young People's Guide to the Adirondacks*. It contains basic information that you should understand, such as how to read maps and use a compass, how to protect the land, and, especially, how to have a safe trip. The most important advice in that book is "never go hiking alone." This applies equally to backpacking--**never go camping alone**. Make sure there is an adult or knowledgeable camper in your group, but you should be the leader in order to gain experience.

The places to camp described in this guide are scattered all over the Adirondack Park, except in the eastern High Peaks where there have been problems of over-use and where new camping regulations may shortly be imposed.

Each of the twenty-five trips described will introduce you to a new region of the park as well as to different types of adventures. Start

with the shorter trips until you feel comfortable carrying a pack and relying on yourself. Use what you learn on the shorter trips to find out just how far you can hike in a day carrying a pack.

There are two groups of trips, those with lean-to destinations and those with only primitive campsites. In each group, the hikes described in this book are arranged in order of difficulty. Along with the descriptions of good places to camp, this book contains simple guidelines for protecting the land and water in the Adirondacks, hints on observing nature, and information on side trips you will want to make from your campsite.

Camping in wild lands is much more complicated than just hiking or camping in a campground. It is hiking to distant places with everything you may need packed in your backpack. You have to be totally self-sufficient and prepare your own meals. Not only do you have to carry everything you may need, you will need special equipment.

You will be living on the land without changing it in any way. There are a few rules and regulations designed to protect the land. These rules exist because in the past there have been careless campers or just too many visitors who have loved the land to death, but you can learn how to camp so that you leave no sign of your visit.

After you have gained experience in camping, you may want to find more camping destinations than are described in this book. Near the end of the book you will find suggestions for camping places where you can use trail descriptions from introductory hiking guides to plan other short camping trips.

This book concludes with a list of longer trips on which you will find lean-tos so you can put together camping expeditions of three to five nights. For these you and your parents or adult companions will need one of the more advanced *Discover the Adirondacks* guides.

*Tying up a
sleeping pad*

Regulations

Camping regulations in the Adirondack Forest Preserve are quite simple. You can camp anywhere on state land, except at places designated with a no-camping sign, for up to three nights, so long as your **campsite is at least 150 feet from water or a trail**. For longer stays and for groups of more than ten people, a permit from the local Department of Environmental Conservation ranger is required. (His or her phone is listed under NYS DEC in local phone books.)

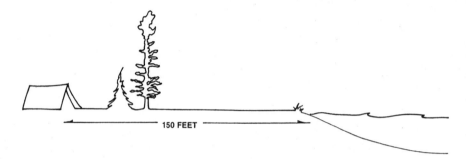

New regulations are being developed for the eastern High Peaks region, but they are not yet finalized. No destinations in this guide are in that over-used area, which needs special protection.

Carry out what you carry in. This means everything from orange peels to candy wrappers. You must not leave garbage behind, and the "Carry-in-Carry-out" policy is one of the most important regulations for preserving wild lands. But, it is equally important to leave no sign of your visit. This guidebook will show you how to camp so that you leave the wild lands as you find them.

Almost all trailheads have **registration books in registration boxes. Always sign in and out.** Always let someone know where you plan to go in case of emergency.

DEC regulations will shortly limit the **size of camping groups** in wilderness areas to twelve because of the damage that can be caused by large camping groups. To preserve a sense of remoteness, you may want to limit your group to four or six, with at least one adult in that number. Two adults in a group of six is ideal--it is a small group but still large enough so everyone can share the loads and the work.

Driving to trailheads

The trips described are located all around the Adirondack Park. Even with the driving instructions given in the text you will want a good driving map. The DeLorme *New York State Atlas and Gazetteer* is the best for roads, and it shows the trails described in this text. The box accompanying each trail description tells where the trailhead is for each excursion and how to drive to the trailhead. The ANCA (Adirondack North Country Association) map is the best sheet map that shows primary and secondary roads.

A driving map or atlas and the maps in this guide are all the maps you will need, unless you plan to do a lot of exploring from your campsite. The box also lists the United States Geological Survey (USGS) quadrangle maps that show the destinations. If you plan to do any additional exploring, you may want to buy some of these quadrangles.

Reading USGS Maps

USGS maps are topographical maps; that means they are drawings that show natural and man-made features. The USGS maps are published by the United States Geographical Survey and are useful for hikers, campers, and canoeists.

The maps that cover the Adirondacks come in two different series. The center of the Adirondack Park has new metric maps; the outlying region is covered by older 7.5-minute maps. The metric maps are twice as big as the 7.5-minute maps and cover about twice the area.

The two kinds of maps have different **scales**. This means that different units of measure on the map are equal to a mile or a kilometer. On the metric maps, 2.5 inches on the map represents a mile. On the 7.5 minute maps, 2.625 inches represents a mile.

Both kinds of maps are colored similarly. Blue lines and blue-colored areas represent water; green represents forested areas; white represents open fields or marshes. Swamps are shown in white with blue-colored designs that represent tufts of grass. Major roads are shown in solid red lines; smaller roads are in dashed red lines. Gravel roads are shown in solid black lines, and trails in dashed black lines.

Different kinds of dashed lines represent boundaries of towns or counties. The metric maps have a key that describes all these features.

It is very important for you to understand the brown curved lines. These are called **contour lines**. Each line connects points that have equal elevation (equal height above sea level). Small brown numbers on those lines tell the elevation. Notice how contour lines form rough concentric circles or ovals that decrease. This shows a hill or mountain and the smallest circle represents the summit. The maps name most mountaintops and give the elevation of some of them. Notice how the circular patterns on some mountains are very irregular. Those forms show valleys and ridges. Contour lines that are close together indicate steeper slopes.

Find the steepest slope on the map. Find the tallest hill.
How many inches represent a mile on this map?

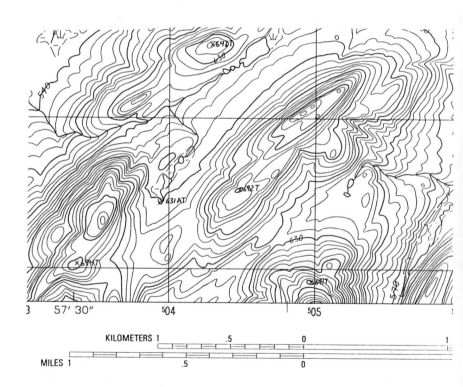

When you are backpacking, you will quickly learn that it is much easier to carry a pack when you are walking on relatively level ground. A few trails in this guide are on fairly steep slopes. You can tell how steep the trails are by seeing how many contour lines are crossed by the dashed line showing the trail. The spaces between the contour lines on a 7.5-minute map represent a 20-foot change in elevation; the spaces on a metric map represent 10 meters, or almost 33 feet. So a trail crossing fifteen contour lines on a metric map is half again as steep as a trail crossing fifteen lines on a 7.5-minute map.

The maps in this guide

Once you've reached the trailhead, the maps in this guide will help you find your destination. However, because these maps are in black and white, it is more difficult to distinguish lakes and streams. All the other features are shown as on the USGS maps. All the maps but two are printed so that true north is at the top of the page. However, in order to fit the copies of the needed maps on the pages of this guide, many of the maps have been reduced from the scale of the USGS. In other words, a smaller measure represents a mile on the map. Accompanying each map is a scale that shows how long a mile is on that map. Look carefully at these scales so you can figure out how the trails differ in length.

Your compass will tell you which way is magnetic north so you line up your map. Your compass is divided into 360 degrees. The arrow points toward magnetic north, 0 or 360 degrees. You need to be able to compute the magnetic direction (MN) you want to take.

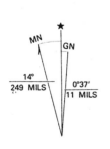

The USGS maps are oriented toward true north ★. Every USGS map has two arrows that indicate the difference between true and magnetic north. In most of the Adirondacks, magnetic north is 14° west of true north. That is why you add 14° to the course you want to take to find the magnetic direction to follow. Or, you subtract 14° from your compass reading to see which direction on the map your route is following.

Equipment

What you should buy

Let's start from the ground up. Since you will be carrying everything you will need, you should have sturdy **hiking boots** that support your ankles. They do not have to be expensive; some of the discount department stores sell rugged boots. Boots should fit and not be too big. Even in summer you will want to wear lightweight wool socks with your boots, so make sure the boots fit comfortably with socks.

Camping equipment is expensive; good camping equipment will last for years. Shop around for the things that will suit you best. Take the advice of stores that specialize in camping and outdoor equipment. Your community may even have a shop that sells recycled camping gear. There are good mail-order catalogs such as L. L. Bean or Campmor.

You will need a **sleeping bag**, a fiber-filled bag that will keep you warm when temperatures drop at night. Choose a bag that is washable, dries quickly, is rated for temperatures down to 40° F., and is as light as possible. Lighter and warmer bags tend to be more expensive. Bags come in many shapes, such as square for extra room or tapered for warmth, and in different lengths to suit your height. You can pair an inexpensive bag with a fleece liner for warmth and

comfort. Just be sure whatever you choose weighs as little as possible and is not too bulky to be rolled into a stuff sack so you can tie it to your backpack. You will be more comfortable if you use a lightweight foam pad. Not only will it make a softer sleeping place, but it will help insulate you from the cold, damp ground.

Sleeping pads range from inexpensive closed-cell foam pads to expensive self-inflating mattresses. Choose something you can afford, but be sure it is light enough to carry.

It is best to have a **backpack** with a built-in frame. It will have a padded belt that can be adjusted to fit snugly on your hips to distribute the weight between your shoulders and your hips. Good padding on the shoulder straps is important, too. Make sure your pack has pockets for different things, so you can quickly find what you need.

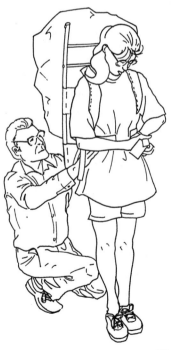

A good backpack will last for years. Some manufacturers, like Tough Traveler (1-800-GO-TOUGH), will repair backpacks if they are kept clean and cared-for. If you have stopped growing, you may want to invest in a full-sized adult pack. If not, perhaps you can borrow one, or find a hand-me-down or secondhand pack.

Rain gear is very important. Always carry a lightweight waterproof poncho or jacket and pants. Gore-Tex or other special fabric rain gear keeps you very dry but it is expensive. For years I used an inexpensive rubberized rain suit, the kind sailors wear. It works even in a downpour.

Be sure to drink plenty of water when you are backpacking.

You will also need
 An unbreakable water
   bottle
 Small flashlight with extra
   batteries
 An emergency whistle
 Your own cup

Personal medicines - Be sure to take any prescription medicines you regularly use such as for asthma or for bee stings if you are allergic to them. One well-stocked medicine kit will serve for your party.

Except for personal things--clothes and so on--everything else you need can be shared. This is very important for two reasons:
Sharing keeps the cost of equipment down, and
Sharing keeps the weight of your pack down.

What you can share

Your **tent** should be as waterproof as possible, with a separate fly and a lightweight frame. The tent should be as light as you can afford. If you plan to travel with just one other person, a two-person tent usually weighs little more than four pounds. If you are planning to camp with three or four people, a larger tent would be better. An outfitter can help you decide.

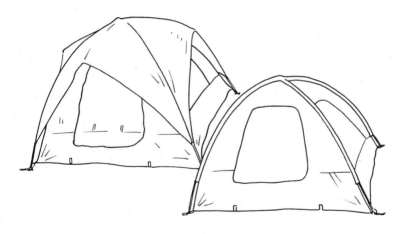

The fly is an extra, outer layer that keeps rain off the tent; the frame is made of flexible rods that support the tent.

Checklist for shared items

_____ A collapsible bucket for carrying water for cooking and washing dishes.

_____ A cookstove and a canister for carrying fuel.

_____ A small cooking kit with a pot, a pot grabber, plates for eating, utensils, and cups. Do not plan to carry much, you will be surprised how little you need.

_____ A filter for purifying water.

_____ A jackknife.

_____ A watertight match container.

_____ Maps and compass.

_____ A small plastic trowel for burying human wastes.

_____ Part of a roll of toilet paper in a sealed plastic bag so it cannot get wet.

_____ A small bottle with biodegradable soap, a small scrubber for washing dishes, a small towel.

_____ A first-aid kit with

aspirin,

safety pins,

cold/hot packs,

cloth Bandaids,

moleskin for blisters,

a small tube of antiseptic cream,

an Ace bandage in case someone gets a sprain.

_____ A small bottle of bug repellent.

_____ A small tube of sunscreen.

_____ Can opener.

_____ A small mirror for signalling should you get lost.

A lightweight nylon sack is good for carrying water for cooking and washing dishes, especially since you are cooking and cleaning up at least 150 feet from water.

Practice lighting your stove and filling it with fuel. Learn how to adjust the pressure of the fuel. The instructions that come with your stove will tell you how to do it.

Carry as few pots, pans, plates and cups as possible. Bring a knife, fork, and spoon for everyone, and don't forget the pot grabber. Your towel can double as a potholder.

Filter enough drinking water so you always have plenty. You can become dehydrated quickly in warm weather when you are hiking, so drink lots of water. Use filtered water for cooking, unless you plan to boil it for at least ten minutes.

Wash and rinse your dishes away from water and dump the waste water in the hole you have dug.

Put toilet paper and all your clothes in separate plastic bags to make sure they do not get wet.

Equipment you can improvise

A ground cloth--It is essential to place a plastic sheet on the ground under your tent as an added protection to keep moisture out. An inexpensive plastic sheet from the hardware store works well.

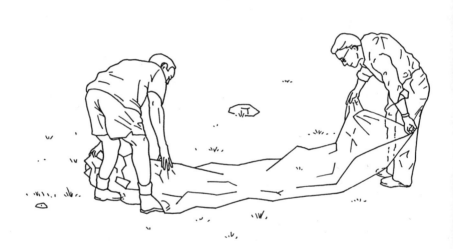

Plastic storage bags--No matter how waterproof your pack is you should put everything in separate plastic bags, then put the bags in your pack to insure everything stays dry. Also, if clothing gets wet when you are wearing it, you can put the damp item in a bag by itself. Food storage or small kitchen waste bags work well.

The hanging bear bag--All your party can share one bag; a large waterproof stuff sack with a drawstring will do. Then you need two lengths of rope, one at least 60 feet long, the other at least 40 feet long. See page 31 for how to hang the bag.

Clothing

Even if you are camping in summer take along a **lightweight wool sweater or fleece jacket.** For an overnight in summer, carry long pants if you are wearing shorts, shorts if you are wearing long pants to start. Take along an extra long-sleeved shirt--it will double as a sleep-shirt. Choose clothing made of or blended with synthetics such as polyesters so they will dry quickly. Cotton clothes soak up moisture and take a long time to dry. Carry a change of underwear, and most important of all, have at least one **change of socks.**

Take along a tiny toothbrush and tube of toothpaste.

Some people like to bring a pair of old sneakers or sandals to wear around camp. Others like to have a bathing suit. Such extras depend on the total weight of your pack and your destination.

When you have your gear assembled, put it on your bathroom scale. The gear for two people on a well-equipped trip should weigh about 30 pounds in each pack. Unless you are nearly full-grown that may be as much as you should carry. Never try to carry more than one-third as much as you weigh; you will have a better trip if your fully loaded pack weighs much less than a third as much as you do.

Things you should <u>not</u> carry in your backpack

Hatchet
Big knife
Glass containers
All-cotton clothes
Radio

Things you should <u>not</u> do

Bother other campers
Build a big fire
Cut trees, shrubs or other vegetation
Dig a trench around your tent
Litter
Make loud disturbances
Disturb wildlife
Stray from camp or your hiking group

Your food

It would be nice to have fresh food because freeze-dried food is not the greatest, but that is not always possible. You need food that does not need to be refrigerated and it has to weigh as little as possible. Experiment at home to see what you like best. If you are going on a single overnight, carry a sandwich to eat for lunch on the way in.

Powdered cocoa and packs of cereal such as instant oatmeal where all you do is add hot water are best for breakfast. I always carry powered orange drink for breakfast as well. Gorp, carrot sticks, granola bars, crackers, pita bread, fruit roll-ups, and hard cheeses can serve for lunch. Dried fruits are especially good. Packets of powdered fruit juices or ice tea make filtered water taste better. If your pack is not too heavy, stick in an apple or an orange.

Freeze-dried meals like spaghetti, macaroni and cheese, whatever you like best can be the basis of your dinner. They are hearty and filling and all you need to do to prepare them is add boiling water.

Dried packaged foods from the grocery store may be more appealing to your taste. Consider soup in a cup, rice and sauce, pasta in a foil pouch, ramen dried noodle soup packages, 5-minute Rice-a-Roni. These have to be cooked but do not require much additional fuel if you add the dried ingredients to water before you bring it to a boil.

Powdered puddings made by simply adding water make a reasonable dessert. Reward yourself with a rich oatmeal cookie.

Peanut butter is rich in energy and keeps well. Carry it in a plastic refillable tube, available at camping stores. Carry crackers or bread in a plastic food box.

These suggestions may not be your favorites, but you will not go hungry, and you will appreciate how light they are. Never carry anything in glass containers. They are heavy and they break.

Don't bring more food than you will need. Estimate the portions the young people and the adults in your party will need. Do not bring anything you won't eat at home. If you have leftovers, remember if you carry it in, carry it out. Apple cores are biodegradable, but orange peels take so long to decompose you should carry them out.

Choosing a campsite

Camp at or near a lean-to, if there is one on your route. Never pitch a tent inside a lean-to.

When you pitch your tent, be sure you:

Choose a level spot.

Choose a place not far from a spring, a stream, or a lake so you will have water; but make sure your campsite is at least 150 feet from any source of water--a stream, river, lakeshore, or spring.

Choose a campsite that is at least 150 feet from any trail.

Sometimes camping spots are designated by a sign as shown below. The same sign with a slash means no camping.

Burying wastes

If there is no outhouse nearby, choose a place back from your tentsite and at least 150 feet from water for your bathroom. With your trowel, dig a hole 10 inches deep and use it for all waste water from washing dishes and brushing teeth as well as for your bathroom. Cover these holes when you leave your campsite. This way the wastes will be broken down by the surrounding soil and not allowed to pollute water sources.

Hanging a bear bag

Careless campers who have left their food or cooking pots around have created a problem in the Adirondacks. Bears are smart. They have learned that campers are a good source of food. In some places bears have become a nuisance, bothering campers. The best way to keep bears away is to hang all your food in a bear bag. If a bear comes near your camp, try to frighten it away by shouting or banging pots or blowing whistles.

To hang a bear bag, search for two sturdy trees about 30 feet apart. Each should have at least one strong branch about 15 or 20 feet from the ground. Wrap one end of the longer rope around a small rock. (We carry a carabiner in one of our pack for this purpose. It is a metal ring that mountain climbers use.) Throw the rock or carabiner attached to the rope over the branch of each tree and fasten the ends so they are as high as possible.

Your second rope goes over the first fixed line. Put all your food and food wrappers in the bear bag or nylon stuff sack. Tie the sack to one end of the second rope and pull on the other end to hoist the bag as high as the cross rope. Tie that end to a tree to keep the bag out of reach of animals.

More on safety

Building a fire

Because you have a stove in your pack, you will not have to build a fire for cooking. So much wood has been removed from around some campsites that the DEC is discouraging campers from building fires. Only build a fire if you get wet and cold and cannot get warm any other way or if you get lost and need to signal searchers. Then, if you do need a fire, make sure you use only dead and downed wood. **Completely drench your fire with water to put it out when you no longer need it.**

Accidents

Accidents can happen. If something happens to one of the people in your group, it is important that at least one person stay with the injured or ill person, while others in your party go for help.

Hypothermia

This guide is intended for summer camping trips only, but even in summer you can get chilled. If you get cold enough your body temperature can drop and you can become confused. This is hypothermia and it can be dangerous. If one of your party gets wet or chilled, give them dry clothes, wrap them in a sleeping bag, and build a fire to help them warm up.

**Extras that are fun
(if there is room in
someone's pack)**
*Small binoculars - for
   wildlife and stargazing
Small star chart
Pocket field guide for
   flowers, birds, bugs
Camera
Notepad
Marshmallows!*

Lean-tos--an Adirondack tradition

In the early nineteenth century, when hunters and explorers first visited the Adirondacks, they began to construct open camps for temporary shelter. These rugged men often became Adirondack guides who carried all the gear and did all the wood-chopping and cooking for visitors to the wild and unsettled region. Adirondack guides built the same kind of open camps for the tourists, often lining the camp floor with balsam boughs to create a soft bed. These three-sided structures had frames made of saplings or poles, walls made of hemlock- or spruce-bark slabs, and sloping roofs covered with evergreen boughs. They were small, low structures, just big enough to protect campers from rain and wind. With his trusty ax, a guide could build such a temporary shelter in little time. Campfires in front of the open shelter warmed campers, dried their clothes, and allowed them to cook their meals. A large log across the front served as a seat.

Some open camps were built for a brief stay, but, gradually, the guides, who mainly traveled along the region's waterways, built more permanent camps beside rivers and lakeshores to use for a whole season or longer. Staying in open camps and living off the land by fishing and hunting was an essential part of early trips into the wilderness.

From this tradition of the guides' open camps came the Adirondack lean-tos, structures built after 1913 by the Conservation Commission for public use. Structures like these lean-tos were not used in other parts of the country, probably because the Adirondacks tends to be both wetter and colder than other parts of the country. Lean-tos are now a distinctive feature of Adirondack backpacking traditions.

Modern lean-tos are sturdily constructed of notched logs with wooden floors. More than fifty lean-tos were built by 1925 and today there are more than 250. These lean-tos are taller than the first open camps and not as deep, making them harder to heat than the guides' camps or shanties.

Most lean-tos were constructed along the Park's canoe routes, such as the Fulton Chain or the Raquette River, or in the High Peaks region. Many were given names of historic figures or pioneering hikers or trail builders. The lean-to destinations in this guide represent those with shorter access trails. They are scattered around so you can discover many different regions of the Park.

Lean-tos are such an important part of Adirondack tradition that they are permitted in the state's wilderness areas, while other structures are not. Many older lean-tos, however, were constructed too close to water. As these deteriorate, they are being replaced at sites at least 150 feet from water.

It's the custom that you share lean-tos with newcomers, clean the site so no one can tell you have been there, and leave a small pile of kindling and logs gathered from dead and downed wood for the next camper.

If lean-tos are full and even if they are not, some campers prefer to tent nearby and use the rocks of the fireplace as a safe place to light a campstove. The deacon's seat--the log placed at the front of a lean-to--makes a good place for sitting.

Because so much wood has been removed from the vicinity of some lean-tos, in the future, fires may only be permitted in emergencies in some heavily used areas. Campers should use portable stoves for cooking. Do not depend on finding a lean-to with space; always carry a tent.

Lean-tos evolved from 19th century guide's shanties like this one.
Courtesy of the Adirondack Museum, Blue Mountain Lake

Destinations with lean-tos

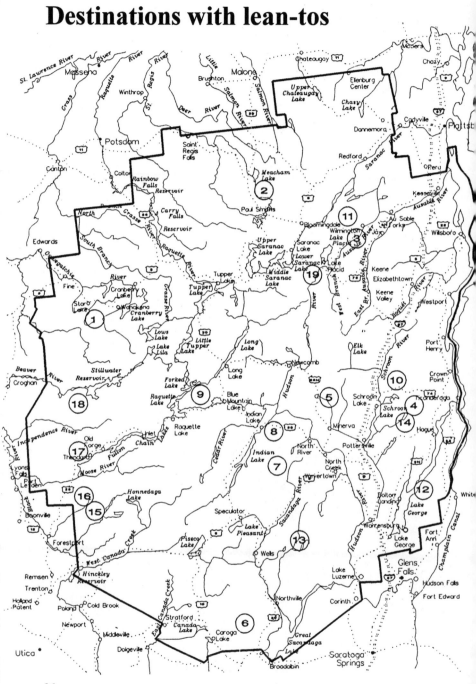

1 - Streeter Lake

Distance - 0.6 mile to the lean-to, 2.7 miles one-way to the Middle Branch Oswegatchie River
Time - ½ hour to the lean-to
Trail markings - Orange snowmobile trail markers
Trailhead - Turn south at the blinking light on NY 3 in the hamlet of Oswegatchie, 2 miles west of Star Lake village. Then turn immediately left; mileages are from this intersection. Turn right at 0.8 mile onto Coffin Mills Road; the turn is before the railroad crossing. Follow that road through Coffin Mills at 2.2 miles and Aldrich at 4 miles. You cross the Oswegatchie River, then at 4.3 miles turn left onto a seasonal dirt road that leads into the Aldrich Pond Wild Forest. Follow this road for 4.5 miles to the former entrance to the Schuler estate. Park here or 0.3 mile farther south at the outlet of Streeter Lake where the continuing roadway (the beginning of the trail) is gated. If you have a canoe, this is a good place to put-in in order to explore Streeter Lake's wooded shores.
USGS Map - Oswegatchie SE

The trail past Streeter Lake and on to the Oswegatchie River passes some very unusual features: fields slowly turning back to forest and side trails to open marshes and bogs, all places you will want to explore. The lean-to on the eastern shore of Streeter Lake can be reached by a very short trail or by canoe, so it is often full. If you cannot camp here, you can continue on the trail south looking for other camping spots and the many other diversions such as bogs and wetlands with wildlife.

This large tract of land, which was sold to the state in 1976, belonged to the Schuler family, whose company produced potato chips. The walk south from the gate starts along an old road through extensive fields where the Schulers once grew seed potatoes in order to develop disease-resistant strains. They brought in Norway and white spruce to replant the fields, exotic trees from other countries.

The lean-to is off to the right at 0.6 mile. The continuing trail reaches a fork at 0.9 mile, go right; at a second fork at 1.1 mile take a short detour right to Crystal Lake. Its clear water and imported sand are great for swimming.

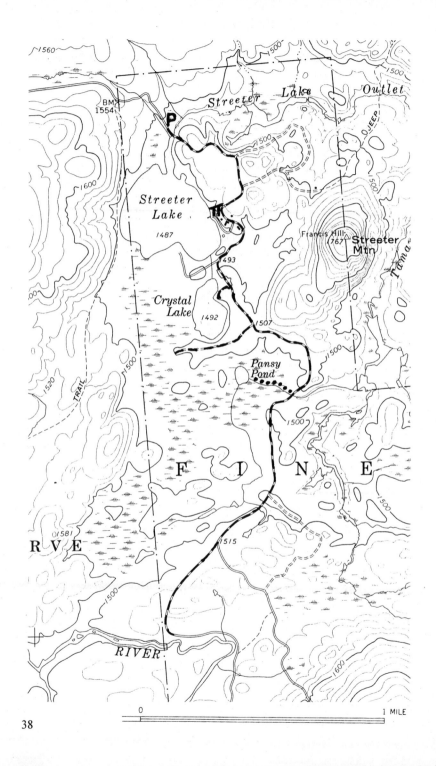

Just beyond the fork to Crystal Lake there is a third fork. Here an overgrown logging road leads you to Streeter Bog. Look for unusual bog plants and Canada jays and three-toed woodpeckers, birds usually found in such wetlands.

If you like to explore bogs, another one is nearby. At 1.6 miles south on the trail you cross the outlet of Pansy Pond. You have to bushwhack along it to find a tiny bog that was created by a receding glacier. Another old road branches from the trail at 1.8 miles. You can detour down it for 0.2 mile to see the pretty wetlands along Tamarack Creek. At 2.7 miles the trail reaches the Middle Branch of the Oswegatchie, where you can find a campsite. Remember to choose one at least 150 feet from the river.

2 - Grass Pond

Distance - 2.1 miles to either lean-to
Time - 1 hour
Trail markings - Yellow horse-trail markers and orange snowmobile trail markers on first half mile, none for remainder
Trailhead - Drive 3.7 miles north on NY 30 from its intersection with Route 192 near Paul Smith's College. Turn right onto a dirt road marked by a DEC sign reading "Hays Brook Assembly Area." Follow it 0.5 mile to a gated side road on the left where the trail begins. Alternately, you can find a place to park back at the 0.3 mile point where the road makes a sharp right-angle turn. A short foot trail beginning halfway between this bend and the gate soon intercepts the main trail.
USGS Map - Saint Regis Mtn.

Until recently Grass Pond was privately owned, yet it has two older lean-tos that were built on its banks by permission of the former owner. Now that it is part of the Forest Preserve, you have the opportunity to enjoy this newer camping destination and see these lean-tos for yourself. Though their construction is similar to others, they certainly have their own personalities.

The main trail follows an old road north through lands devastated by major forest fires almost ninety years ago. Many areas were reforested with straight rows of pines that now tower high above you. In just over 0.5 mile the trail drops to cross the Osgood River, which was a popular fishing attraction for tourists over a century ago.

On the other side of the river, the marked trail continues on to Hays Brook, but you should look for an old road coming in on your right. This is the way to Grass Pond, and though it may not yet have any markers, it is an easy route to follow. It climbs steadily over higher ground, then drops to cross the Grass Pond outlet.

In just under 2.0 miles, you will come to a clearing with stacks of decaying logs on the right. The route turns left here and splits just after reentering the trees. Turning right, you quickly arrive at the brushy edge of Grass Pond. A steep hill rises up on your right and if you look carefully through the trees, you will see a lean-to perched high up on a flat area. A sign on its wall calls it the Hidden Pond lean-to and there is no well-worn path to it. The lean-to has a dirt

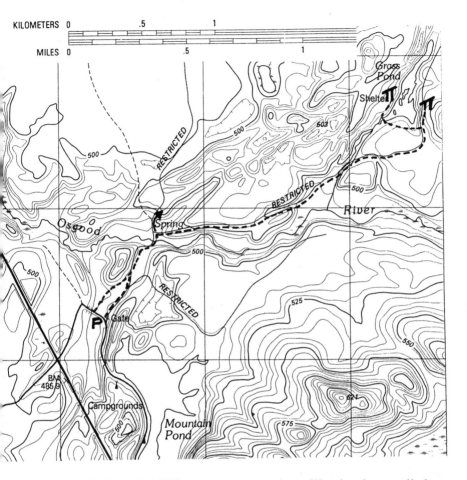

floor and since the hill is so steep, a wooden railing has been nailed to the trees directly in front of it.

If you turn left at the junction, you will cross the pond's outlet, then come to the second, and better-located, lean-to. It too has a dirt floor as well as two wooden chairs and end tables, but its most unusual feature is a wood stove! With all these furnishings it is difficult to find enough room to spread out your sleeping bag, but there is ample room nearby to pitch your tent. A wooden plaque inside the lean-to tells you that it was "Constructed by Mr. Weigel's Forest Recreation Class, Summer of 1971." Those students from Paul Smith's College must have really enjoyed that assignment!

3 - Copperas Pond

Distance - 0.5 mile one-way to the lean-to, more if you explore the other two ponds
Time - Forty minutes
Trail markings - Blue with red and yellow on side trips
Trailhead - From its intersection with NY 73 Lake Placid, drive 6.4 miles northeast on NY 86 to a turnout on the left. The trail begins on the right. This is 2.8 miles south of the entrance to the Whiteface Mountain Ski Center.
USGS Map - Lake Placid

Copperas Pond sits in a rocky bowl on the shoulder of the massive Sentinel Range. The trail to it is very steep, but so short that it is well worth the effort of carrying a full backpack up to enjoy a weekend on its beautifully wooded shores. This is a good place to camp so you can walk to two other small ponds nearby.

From the register, you climb up a narrow draw to a junction, 0.2 mile from the highway. You will gain 200 feet in this stretch and the rocks can be slippery, so use care and take your time. The red trail ahead goes on toward Winch Pond, a side trip described below.

Turn right at the junction, following the blue markers up a final pitch and then down to the pond. A sparsely marked side trail to the right winds through trees and rocks to the lean-to. There are plenty of boulders at the water's edge from which to swim, picnic or just relax and enjoy the scenery. With so many different kinds of trees to be found, it is fun to see who can pick out the cedars, spruce, birch, pine, hemlock, and beech.

The blue trail continues south around Copperas Pond, reaching a junction with a yellow trail that heads northeast to Winch Pond. Though it is only 0.5 mile long, the trail leads through a tall, peaceful forest where the feeling of wilderness is strong. Winch Pond itself seems most wild with Stewart Mountain reflected in its lilypad-filled waters. Just before reaching the pond, the red trail seen earlier on your climb up from the highway comes in on your left. To return to your campsite, you can take this trail as a loop, turning left when you reach the blue trail, or retrace your steps along the yellow trail. Either way totals just over a mile in length.

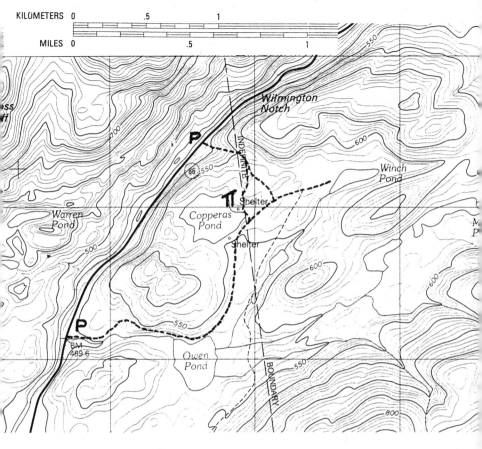

Back at Copperas Pond, continue on the blue trail past the yellow trail junction. You will cross the pond's outlet then reach the site of a former lean-to where there is a spectacular view across the water to Whiteface Mountain. It is a good spot for a picnic and for picture taking.

From here, the trail swings south and descends through deep forest to Owen Pond, 0.6 mile away. Its waters reflect the soaring flanks of Kilburn Mountain, one of the highest peaks in the Sentinel Range. Turning right, the trail follows the edge of the pond, then descends along its outlet to the highway, 0.7 mile away. This can serve as an alternate hike out to a second vehicle or, if you are careful, for a mile-long walk north along the highway to your parking spot.

4 - Grizzle Ocean

Distance - 1.9 miles one-way
Time - 1½ to 2 hours
Trail markings - Blue and yellow
Trailhead - Putnam Pond Campground (there may be a day-use fee for parking). Head south from NY 74, 13.3 miles east of Northway Exit 28 or 4.9 miles west of NY 22 in Ticonderoga. The campground is 3.6 miles south of NY 74. Follow signs to the parking area.
USGS Map - Graphite, NY

There are so many wonderful ponds to visit in the Pharaoh Lake Wilderness Area that it is difficult to pick just one. Some have good swimming beaches, others have beautiful rock ledges along their shores, some have good fishing, and every place is different. Grizzle Ocean has a short enough trail that its lean-to and campsites are often full; many people agree that this is a very attractive place. Because of this, it is best to plan a midweek camping trip. Grizzle Ocean has both swimming and fishing, and you can enjoy climbing on the steep rocky slopes that line the southwest side of the pond. Since you are sure to like the area, you may want to extend your visit by walking all around Putnam Pond; there are lean-tos at Rock and Little Rock ponds, which you pass on the well-marked route that circles Putnam Pond. You can also climb Treadway Mountain on a trail that forks from that circuit trail. But, for a first trip, head to Grizzle Ocean. Lore has it that the pond's funny name came from an old logger who bragged so much about the huge numbers of fish he caught there that his friends called it Grizzle's Ocean.

From the parking area, the trail heads south along the shore of Putnam Pond, but back from it. Shortly after you start hiking you cross a bridge. At 0.15 mile there is a fork to the pond, a second bridge, and a sharp rise up a ridge. At 0.85 mile the trail descends the ridge to a bridge over the outlet of Berrymill Pond; there are lovely waterfalls upstream. Your only view of Putnam Pond is in the next 0.1 mile.

At 1 mile you cross a bridge and still another one at 1.35 miles, this one the outlet of Grizzle Ocean. Just beyond this bridge there is an intersection. The yellow trail right leads to a fork to Treadway

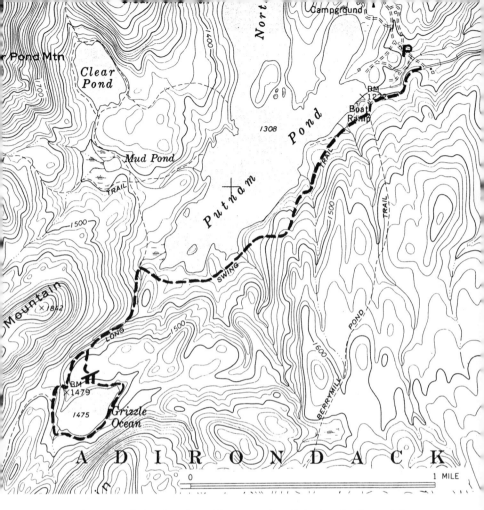

Mountain or straight ahead to Clear Pond and the beginning of the circuit of Putnam Pond. You want to turn left, also on a yellow-marked trail, which climbs steadily to recross the outlet of Grizzle Ocean at 1.6 miles. At 1.7 miles, the trail forks again. The yellow trail heads south toward Pharaoh Lake; turn left on the blue trail for 0.3 mile to the Grizzle Ocean lean-to.

The blue trail makes a 1.1 mile circuit of the pond, passing several campsites. It is close to shore most of the time and occasionally wet. Making a clockwise circuit, near the outlet, a yellow trail forks left toward Pharaoh Lake. To complete the circuit, stay right (also yellow-marked) to walk through a deep hemlock grove before returning to the intersection with the main trail.

45

5 - Stony Pond

Distance - 2 miles one-way, moderate climb
Time - 1 to 1½ hours
Trail markings - Orange snowmobile trail markers
Trailhead - The east side of NY 28 N, 3.8 miles north of the intersection of county route 30 in Minerva.
USGS Maps - Schroon Lake and Dutton Mtn.

Stony Pond is a destination on a hub of trails leading to four other small ponds. The lean-to at Stony Pond is located so you can spend a full day of exploring these trails and ponds when you camp here for two nights. Stony itself is quite pretty, and you can find a place to swim along the west shore.

The trail follows an old road so it is easy to find and walk the trail. Five minutes from the trailhead you reach an unmarked intersection. The way right leads to state land on the shore of Twenty-ninth Pond.

A beaver chewed this tree.

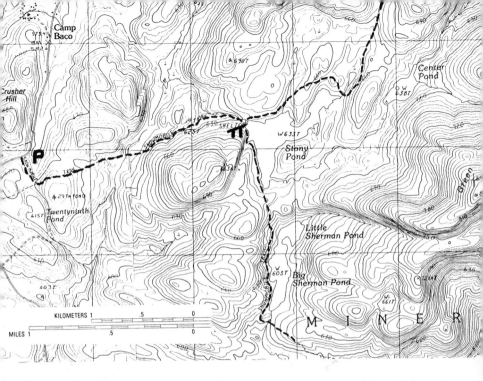

The way left climbs, levels off, climbs to a high spot, and descends to Stony Pond. The lean-to is in an open field with plenty of room for tent camping. The pretty, evergreen shores frame a view across to Green Mountain.

Trails lead both northeast and south along the shore of the pond. If you go northeast, then east, there are interesting wetlands and, a little more than 0.25 mile past the northeast tip of the pond, there is a small, yellow-marked trail that leads to Center Pond, a tiny, marshy pond with wildflowers that include carpets of creeping white winterberry.

Heading south from the lean-to, the trail climbs the steep slopes of Stony Pond's western shore, then descends to a small marsh beneath a tall, vertical rock face. Red markers here help you find your way around flooding from a temporary beaver pond. The trail south climbs to a height-of-land, then descends to Big and Little Sherman ponds, with their steep-sloped western shores. Beaver have flooded these ponds, forcing a route away from the old road. The trail hugs the steep slopes of Big Sherman Pond all the way to the narrow outlet.

6 - Chase Lake

Distance - 2.6 miles one-way
Time - 1½ hours
Trail markers - Yellow and red
Trailhead - Parking area at the end of Pinnacle Road. Drive north on NY 10 and 29A in Caroga Lake, turn right, east, on Fulton County Route 112, the Benson Road. At 6.6 miles from NY 10, turn north on Pinnacle Road and continue for 2.8 miles to the parking area.
USGS Maps - Jackson Summit and Caroga Lake

A relatively short and very level trail leads to a seldom-used lean-to at Chase Lake in the southern Adirondacks. There is good birding from the lean-to area and on the way in, but it is difficult to fish the lake without a boat. The lean-to is situated on a small knoll between two swampy areas, so it is not easy to walk around the shores of the lake, which are quite interesting. So consider this backpack a challenge to see if, by sharing loads, someone in your party can also carry a small inflatable boat. The Adirondacks is filled with many backpack destinations to distant lakes that are best enjoyed with a lightweight boat. If you have one, you can fish, explore the small gorge around the outlet, enjoy the far northwest shore and the views of the formidable cliffs on Pinnacle Mountain northwest of the lake.

The trail traces a winding route to the lake in order to avoid private land and follows different old logging roads. A wetland borders the parking area. A narrow path leads beside it on the left, north, for 200 yards to the first of these roads. Turn left, northeast, on it and at 0.4 mile, the marked route angles east on a narrower trail. This trail curves southeast around the private land, then heads almost south down two small slopes. There is a bridge over a small stream at the bottom of the second slope, then a short rise, and the trail intersects a red-marked trail coming in from private land. The red and yellow trails proceed together for another 0.2 mile. At about 1 mile from the start, the yellow trail turns left, northeast.

The forest is now much higher with tall hemlocks filling the draw to your right. A stream draining this draw is an inlet of Chase Lake. You cross two small streams that flow into the inlet stream, then at

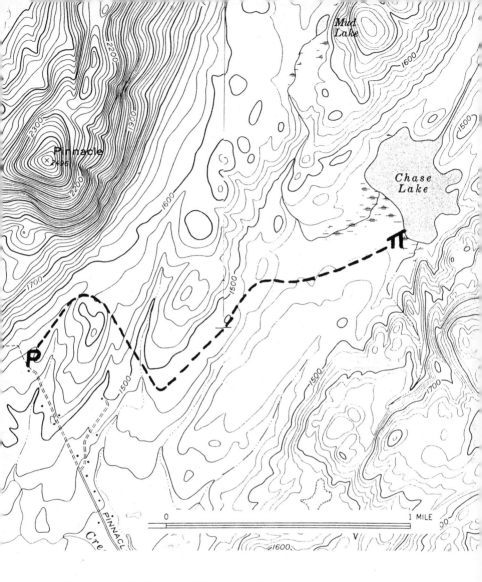

1.8 miles, cross the inlet itself. The trail is now almost due east and level except for a small descent at the final approach to the lake.

The lean-to and its picnic table make a good place to practice cooking a meal. If you have enough time, you should explore beyond the lean-to because visitors who see the lake only from the lean-to are often disappointed. If you do not have an inflatable boat, try walking counter-clockwise around the shore to the outlet by first circling south of the marshy area to the east of the lean-to.

7 - Puffer Pond

Distance - 2 miles one-way, 600-foot climb
Time - 1½ hour
Trail markings - Red
Trailhead - Puffer Pond's western trail shares a private trailhead with Chimney Mountain. The trailhead, at Kings Flow, is on private land and there is a small parking fee. To reach Kings Flow, drive to the end of Big Brook Road, which forks east from NY 30 0.5 mile south of NY 28 in Indian Lake village. Big Brook Road crosses Abanakee Lake causeway and forks right where Starbuck Road (Wilderness Lodge) continues straight. Big Brook Road continues south to reach Kings Flow almost 8 miles from NY 30. The parking area beside the field is marked.
USGS Map - Thirteenth Lake

Puffer Pond attracts fishermen, so you may want to bring along fishing gear--if you are lucky you may have fish for breakfast. Other than fishermen, the pond has few visitors. Two lean-tos are sited about 0.5 mile apart on the north shore. The long, thin pond is nestled between Puffer and Bullhead mountains, high in the northern portion of the Siamese Ponds Wilderness Area. Two trails lead to it; both involve some climbing.

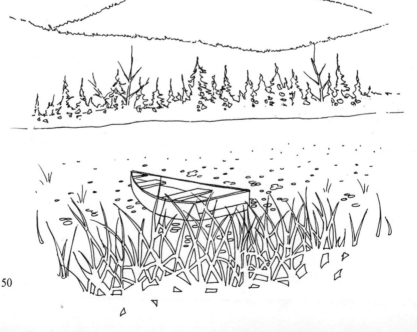

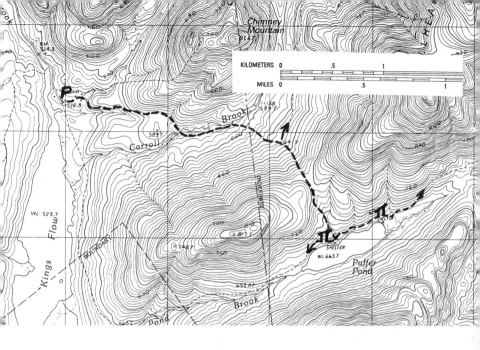

From the parking area for the western trail, head east across the field and enter the woods on an old road, immediately cross a bridge, and continue to the registration booth at the edge of state land. The trail follows the valley of Carroll Brook with its wetlands and many beaver flows. Watch for markers that direct you across the brook on a beaver dam. This section of trail is especially pretty and rich in wildlife. The trail follows the south side of the beaver flows, then gradually heads uphill to a sharp right-angle turn at 1.2 miles. The sign directs you to turn right to Puffer Pond. (A faint blue-marked trail heads north here toward the John Pond Road.)

The red trail heads up steeply to a height-of-land, then descends sharply down 200 feet in a very short distance on rocky outcrops to the western lean-to on the shore of Puffer Pond. The trail continues east following the shore, but not close to it, to the eastern lean-to. Fishermen use the boats left at the pond; if you find one that is not locked, make sure it does not leak and remember the fisherman's code--return it exactly as you find it.

If you return early enough from your overnight at Puffer, you may want to climb Chimney Mountain. The climb up should take about an hour and a half. Be careful near the rock cliffs and ledges and the cave openings.

8 - John Pond

Distance - 2.8 miles one-way
Time - 1½ to 2 hours
Trail markings - Blue
Trailhead - Turn east on Big Brook Road, which forks from NY 30 just south of Indian Lake Village. The road goes over Abanakee causeway. Start measuring from the end of it and continue to a fork at 1.8 miles, where Big Brook Road turns south. Go left here and in left again in a couple hundred yards onto Starbuck Road. Starbuck Road reaches a T at 3 miles; turn right for 0.25 mile to the parking area for John Pond.
USGS Map - Thirteenth Lake

You can swim and laze about at John Pond, but the best reason for camping there is so you will have time to explore the cliffs, ledges, and views from the mountain that lies west of the pond. John Pond is a popular destination, accessible along a trail that follows a road that was open to vehicles until recent years. The first 1.7 miles to the boundary of the Siamese Ponds Wilderness Area is heavily rutted, but the walk is easy. Unless it has been very wet so the ruts hold water, the hike is quite pleasant.

The road borders marshes as it heads south, then gradually angles west. Stop to enjoy the views south over the marshes. One opening reveals the chimney on Chimney Mountain; another, at the end of a side path, looks off to Bullhead Mountain. The road crosses the Hamilton-Warren County line at 2.5 miles.

A short distance beyond the boundary, a short path leads north to an old cemetery. Just before the trail begins to rise, there is a fork to the right, south, marked with yellow ski-trail markers and blue. It leads in 3.7 miles to the Puffer Pond trail (page 50), along a beautiful, little-used, and sometimes hard-to-follow, deep woods trail.

The John Pond trail rises slightly through a pleasant area that has been reforested with evergreens, now fully grown. The trail crosses John Pond Outlet, then continues on the level to the pond. The lean-to is usually occupied on weekends and often during midweek. Walk north along the east shore to find several other good camping spots.

Walk around the pond, looking for wildflowers and unusual plants. Under the trees you can find many different ground covers,

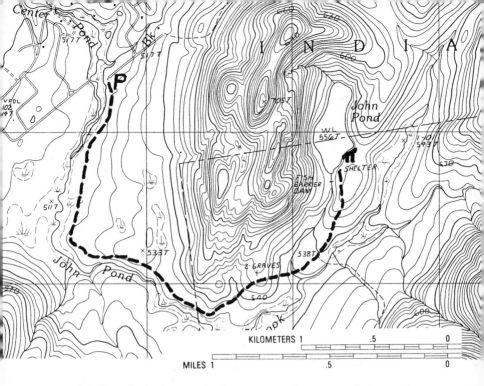

ground cedar, pipsissiwa, and wintergreen. If you can circle north around the pond you can find a cleft on the west shore that leads up to the exposed rock ledges on John Pond Mountain. Be careful choosing your way; be sure that if you climb a ledge that there is a way back down. A series of lookouts from the top of the ledges gives you ever-expanding views that become more and more spectacular as you ascend. You are always within sight of the pond, so you will have no trouble returning to your campsite. But, be careful to choose a safe route down the steep slopes. The view south toward Chimney Mountain is great but the best view is east over the range of steep summits that includes Peaked Mountain, with the High Peaks visible in the distance beyond.

This overnight can be combined with the Puffer Pond trip for a three-day circuit, but for this you will need the USGS map. Note that the trail connecting the John and Puffer Pond trails is seldom walked (most people use it as a ski trail). You have to look carefully for the markers because there is no foot tread or visible footpath along much of the way. Still, it is a fine trail through great forest stands with glimpses of the steep slopes of Chimney Mountain.

9 - Sargent Ponds

> **Distance** - 6.9 mile loop, plus 1.6 miles along North Point Road
> **Time** - 5 hours, although either pond can be reached in an hour or so.
> **Trail markings** - Orange snowmobile markers and red trail markers
> **Trailhead** - Drive west on North Point Road from NY 30. Bear left at the fork where the way right leads to Forked Lake Campground. The trailhead for Upper Sargent Pond is 6.3 miles from NY 30, the trailhead for Lower Sargent Pond is at 7.9 miles.
> **USGS Maps** - Forked Lake and Raquette Lake

Upper Sargent Pond has some of the best swimming in the central Adirondacks. Lower Sargent Pond has a lean-to. Both have good fishing and several good campsites and no matter where you camp, there are plenty of places to explore and things to do. You have your choice of approach trails. This guide describes a loop using both, but note that their trailheads are 1.6 miles apart on the North Point Road.

The trail to Upper Sargent Pond is 1.3 miles long, with a gentle ascent, then a long descent to a trail junction. Straight ahead there is a campsite opposite an island. Other campsites can be found along the shore of this long thin pond.

The direct approach to Lower Sargent Pond is 2.1 miles long. The trail climbs slightly, then levels before reaching Grass Pond at 1.3 miles. The trail follows the pond's western shore, then curves around the southern end before heading south along a marshy inlet stream. At 2 miles, you reach a three-way intersection. The way left, east, leads you in 1.7 miles northeast to the intersection near Upper Sargent Pond. The way right crosses a wet area and two plank bridges in 0.1 mile before reaching a second three-way intersection. The way left, east, circles for 0.2 mile around a part of the northern shore of Lower Sargent Pond to a lean-to on a pine-covered point. The way right quickly crosses the outlet on a bridge near a dam on the outlet.

From the junction, the main trail heads south along the shore of the pond, although the trail is not close to the pond. The trail then turns right, west, away from Lower Sargent Pond and heads for Tioga Point on Raquette Lake. If you plan to camp over for two nights, consider making this long walk (8 miles round-trip) to Tioga Point

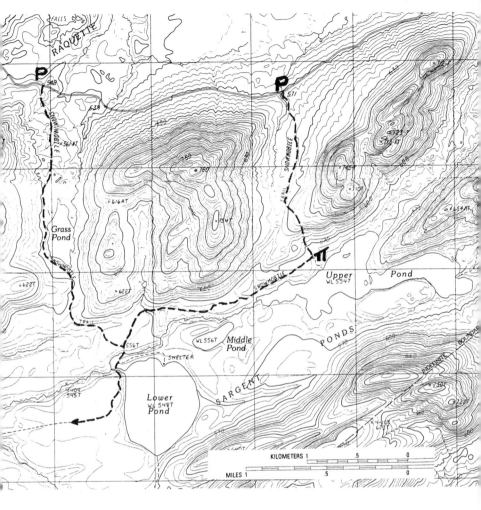

one of your side trips. This little-used trail is sometimes faint, so be sure you have a USGS map and compass. The trail leads past lovely marshes filled with bird life to a peninsula where there is good swimming.

There is a second approach to Lower Sargent Pond where you might camp. This one, an unmarked path, forks east from the Tioga Point trail at the place where that trail makes a sharp right-angle turn away from the pond, about a third of a mile south of the dam over the outlet of Lower Sargent Pond.

10 - Moose Mountain Pond

Distance - 3.1 miles one-way
Time - 2 to 2½ hours
Trail markings - Blue
Trailhead - A parking lot on the south side of the Essex County Route 4, the North Hudson to Moriah road. Take Northway Exit 29 east for 0.3 miles to NY 9. At 2.6 miles turn right on Old Route 9 and turn right again in 0.3 mile onto County Route 4. Measuring from this last intersection, the parking lot is 2.8 miles east.
USGS Map - Paradox Lake

The lean-to at Moose Mountain Pond in the Hammond Pond Wild Forest is a wonderful destination. The tiny little pond is remote and quiet and you will want to explore its shore for plants and frogs. The access trail is varied and long enough to give you a taste for a more extensive backpack trip. Your trail leaves from the right or west side of the parking area. It starts out following an old road that is closed to vehicular traffic.

After 0.3 mile the trail turns right, heading away from the old roadbed to higher ground above a marsh. You follow the edge of the marsh then return to follow the old road again. Watch for the beginning and end of this detour that keeps you out of wet ground.

At 0.6 mile the trail rises slightly following Berrymill Brook. There is a small waterfall on the brook at 0.9 mile, a good place to stop and rest. Beyond, the trail climbs again to a height-of-land at 1.3 miles. There is a cedar grove at the bottom of the next short downslope. Here at 1.5 miles a yellow-marked trail forks right, west, to Bass Lake, a possible side trip.

Beyond the intersection, the blue trail turns west on a bridge over the outlet of Berrymill Flow. It is a pretty place with camping spots nearby. You can enjoy a rest stop here and explore the edges of the long marsh that stretches out to the south. A beaver dam that used to hold water in the flow is just upstream from the bridge. Berrymill hardly deserves the name pond (as is shown on the map) because it is now just a long, wet marsh.

The blue trail continues on the east side of Berrymill Flow, but back from it for 0.4 mile until you cross a bridge over a stream that

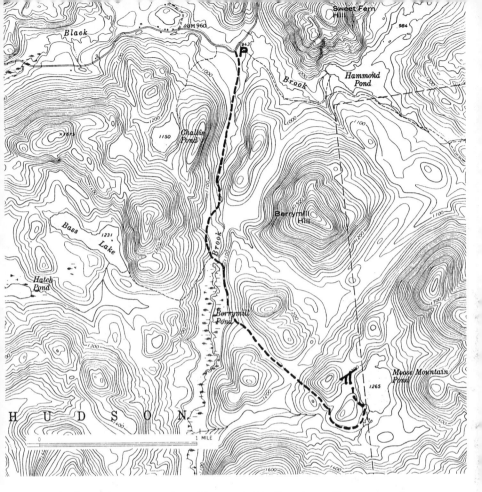

only flows in wet weather. Here at 1.9 miles the trail turns southeast away from the flow, following a creek bed between two small hills, then winds through open woods. The trail splits and rejoins, then at 2.5 miles splits again. The way left disappears in a marsh. The way right heads up along a hillside, then along a marshy area and through a beautiful pine and hemlock stand. At 2.9 miles you can see the outlet brook of Moose Mountain Pond. At the outlet, the trail turns north along the west shore, past a campsite that looks out at Moose Mountain. At 3.1 miles you reach the lean-to, which also enjoys views of the rugged slopes that surround the pond.

For other trips nearby, try the short trail to Challis Pond, which begins 150 yards west of the parking area, or the trail that starts on the east side of the parking area and leads to Hammond Pond.

11 - Cooper Kill Pond

Distance - 2.7 miles one-way, 870 feet elevation change, with some very steep sections
Time - 3 hours
Trail markings - Red
Trailhead - Head west toward Whiteface Mountain on County Route 431 from the four corners in Wilmington and bear right at 2.9 miles onto County Route 18, which leads toward Franklin Falls. Pass the beginning of the Whiteface Memorial Highway, and at 3.6 miles the trailhead for Cooper Kill Pond is on the right.
USGS Map - Wilmington

The new USGS metric map calls this Cooper Kill Pond, but trailhead signs and local custom call it Cooperkiln Pond. The pond is a tiny, rock-dotted gem nestled high on the shoulder of the Stephenson Mountain Range. The 870-foot ascent in 2.7 miles is steeper and involves more climbing than any other trail described in this guide. Consider this trip a challenge and good experience for future camping among the Adirondack's higher peaks.

The beauty of camping at the lean-to at Cooper Kill Pond in the Stephenson Range is that this is a little-known and not heavily used destination. The trail starts along an old logging road which is well marked, though it's sometimes wet. You pass several small streams,

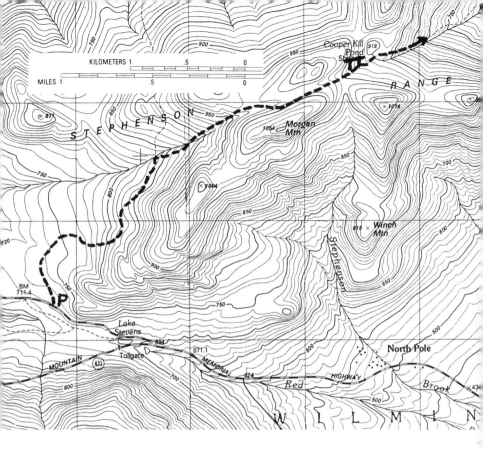

then at 1.2 miles cross over two log bridges. Stop and rest here because the steady climb continues. The trail turns more easterly to follow French Brook, which is in a steep valley on your left, north. The trail levels as it approaches a meadow that is the headwaters of the brook.

The trail reaches a height-of-land at 2 miles. The summit of Morgan Mountain is to your right and only 175 feet higher than the high point of the trail. The trail begins a gradual descent, follows a small stream, then crosses it to reach the inlet 220 feet below the height-of-land. Cross the inlet on logs, follow around the shore to the outlet, and cross it, again on logs, before reaching the lean-to.

The trail continues down to the northeast. This trail that follows Pettigrew Brook begins its steep descent near the lean-to. This is a lovely trail, but not recommended for the backpack to Cooper Kill Pond because it has even more vertical ascent than the trail described.

12 - Fishbrook Pond

Distance - 4.3 miles one-way, moderate climbing
Time - 3 hourss
Trail markings - Red, yellow, and blue
Trailhead - From NY 22 south of Ticonderoga or north of Whitehall, find Clemons, where you turn west toward Huletts Landing. Turn south on Pike Brook Road, 2.6 miles west of NY 22 and go 0.8 mile to a marked trailhead, the same trailhead as for Black Mountain fire tower.
USGS Maps - Shelving Rock and Whitehall, NY

Black Mountain is the tallest of the peaks in the beautifully forested range of mountains that lie along the east shore of Lake George. Hidden among them are some wonderful trails and destinations. A half dozen tiny ponds are nestled high in this range. There are four lean-tos on these ponds, two of which are on Fishbrook Pond, which has great swimming. This is a longer walk that offers several side trips. All these advantages add up to a good reason to visit this area for at least a two-night stay.

The red-marked portion of the trail begins along a gravel road that leads 0.7 mile to a private residence. The trail follows the right side of some fields up into the woods and at 1 mile reaches a fork. The red trail continues up Black Mountain--one of the side excursions you may want to consider--but for now turn south on the blue trail.

The trail, still following an old road, passes a bog, climbs over a hemlock knoll, crosses a bridge, then at 1.5 miles enters a draw. The next 0.6 mile to Lapland Pond is level but often wet. There is an intersection at the north end of the pond. The way left leads to Lapland Pond's lean-to on top of a rock ledge about a third of the way down the pond's eastern shore. It's a wonderful spot to stop for a swim.

The blue trail continues south for 0.2 mile to an intersection. The way right is the yellow-marked segment to Black Mountain ponds. A detour west for 1.6 miles leads to a pleasant picnic spot on the steep slopes of the western pond.

The way south is also marked yellow. The trail leads past stump-filled wetlands, passes a left fork that leads to a snowmobile trailhead on private land, then, 0.5 mile from the intersection, begins to climb

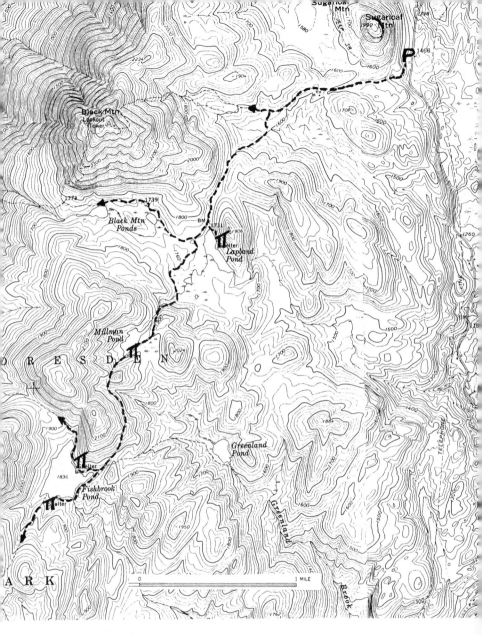

as it continues south. The grade is moderate as the trail crosses the outlet of Millman Pond twice. Emerging from a narrow draw, the trail reaches Millman Pond and continues on a narrow ridge east of the narrow pond. To the east of the ridge lies a beaver meadow and a lean-to with a fireplace sits on top of the ridge.

South of Millman Pond, the trail climbs 100 feet to a saddle, then descends 200 feet to Fishbrook Pond in a mile. Just before reaching the pond, a red trail forks east toward Greenland Pond. Just beyond that junction, there is a second intersection, with the way right leading 0.2 mile to the northern lean-to and on to the northern corner of the pond. That lean-to sits high on a rock ledge that slopes gradually to shore, a fine place to swim. The way left, along the eastern shore, leads to another nice lean-to on the southern corner of the pond.

This would be a good trip for practicing map-reading skills with a real topographic map. From the pond, you can make a day trip south to Bumps Pond, followed by a loop over Sleeping Beauty. For this you need the Shelving Rock USGS map or a guidebook to help you sort out the various intersections.

13 - Wilcox Lake

Distance - 4.8 miles one-way from the south; 4.7 miles from the west
Time - 3 hours or more for either approach
Trail markings - Orange snowmobile trail markers
Trailhead - The southern trailhead is at the end of Stony Creek Road north of Hope Falls. From NY 30 at Hope, 0.5 mile north of the bridge over the Sacandaga River, drive east to Hope Falls and turn north on Stony Creek Road.
   The western or Willis Lake trailhead is at the end of Pumpkin Hollow Road, which also heads east from NY 30 about 4 miles north of Hope. This road leads past Wilcox Lake to a parking area near Doig Creek, 3.4 miles from NY 30.
USGS Maps - Harrisburg and Hope Falls

Wilcox Lake gave its name to the huge wild forest area that surrounds it. The lake has beautiful shores and to the northwest a rugged mountain vista. Wilcox Lake has two lean-tos on the south shore and several good campsites on its western shore. Almost as attractive as the lake itself are two of its three access trails. You will find them as wonderful deep woods walks as any in the Adirondacks.

It is also a very popular lake with fishermen, partly because there is one short access route to it along an extension of the road from Stony Creek to Harrisburg Lake. This route crosses private land and four-wheel-drive vehicles can drive as far as the stream crossing at Bakertown. I prefer one of the other two approaches, both of which follow long-abandoned old roads. They may be a little longer and harder than the route from Harrisburg Lake because the trails are steeper, but they are both so attractive it is hard to choose one. If you can arrange to be dropped off at one trailhead and picked up at the other, you can walk both in a great loop. Walk in on the trail from the south and out via Willis Lake. Approaching Wilcox Lake via Willis Lake involves much more uphill walking.

If you choose the Willis Lake trailhead, the trail descends for 0.2 mile to the bridge over Doig Creek, then begins a fairly steep climb to a height-of-land at 0.7 mile. Beyond, the trail winds about on high ground, then at 1.3 miles begins a gentle descent. The trail now heads downhill, then up and down, and at 2.5 miles crosses a tributary of Wilcox Outlet. The trail is now in the valley of Wilcox Lake Outlet,

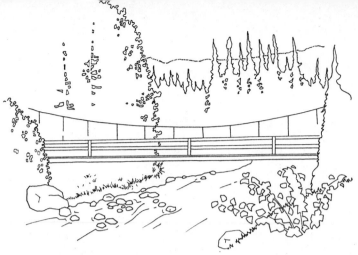

and the forest through which you walk is one of the most wonderful old-growth hardwood stands in the Adirondacks. At 3.5 miles, you cross the Wilcox Outlet stream on a newly rebuilt bridge. (If it washes out again, this crossing can be very difficult in high water.) After crossing the outlet, the trail begins to climb again, a steady 400-foot rise along the slopes of Wilcox Mountain. From the height-of-land, the trail passes a trail leading east and sharply down to the valley of the East Stony Creek. Continue straight ahead to the lean-to.

To get to Wilcox Lake from the south, park at the designated spot and walk north for 200 yards to the snowmobile bridge over Tenant Creek. This stretch is private land; state land begins a bit north of the bridge. The trail swings east then back north, following a relatively level route through a valley. At 1.2 miles you reach Stony Creek and curve east to follow it. It will be on your left until you reach the bridge over Stony Creek at 4.1 miles. Sometimes you are close enough to see water, sometimes you are on high slopes above it so you only hear it. In this long stretch, the trail rises 200 feet, passing first an unnamed creek, then, at 3.3 miles from the start, Dayton Creek. At 4.1 miles, cross the snowmobile bridge where you begin another 200-foot climb to the height-of-land south of the lake. Turn right, north, to the lean-to and a view across to New Lake Mountain.

The eastern shore is wet and marshy, but you can explore the western shore as far as the outlet and sometimes find a log or beaver dam to help you across the outlet. The northwestern shore is drier and quite pretty.

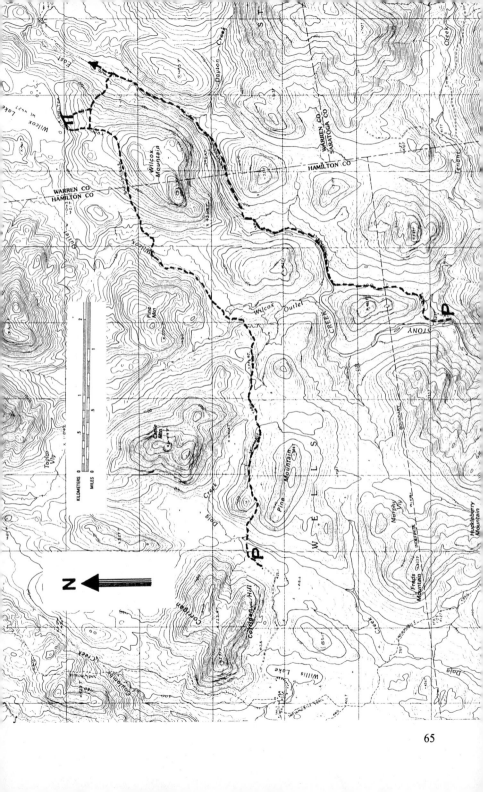

65

14 - Pharaoh Lake

Distance - 3.5 miles to the lake, varied distances to campsites
Time - Allow 3 hours or more to reach a camping destination
Trail markings - Blue
Trailhead - Drive east from Northway Exit 25 on NY 8 to Palisade Road. Turn north and follow the road as it curves around the northern bays of Brant Lake. Turn north on Beaver Pond Road, which is 1.6 miles from NY 8, and turn right again, north, onto Pharaoh Lake Road 3.1 miles from NY 8. Continue to a trailhead 0.4 mile down this road. There are also parking turnouts nearby.
USGS Maps - Pharaoh Mtn. and Graphite, NY

It's intriguing to imagine why the name of ancient Egyptian rulers was given to Pharaoh Lake, but the namer certainly had Egypt in mind, because farther north in the wilderness area is a Pyramid Lake.

Pharaoh Lake entices the camper with its sheer beauty, the rock ledges along its shores, the outcrops and evergreens that frame mountain views, the water lily-filled bays, and ever-changing vistas of its many islands and Pharaoh Mountain which looms over the lake to the northwest. The lake is over 2 miles long with many miles of shore. There is enough to see that you may want to plan a three- or four-night camping trip, but because the lake is so popular, try to plan your trip for weekdays.

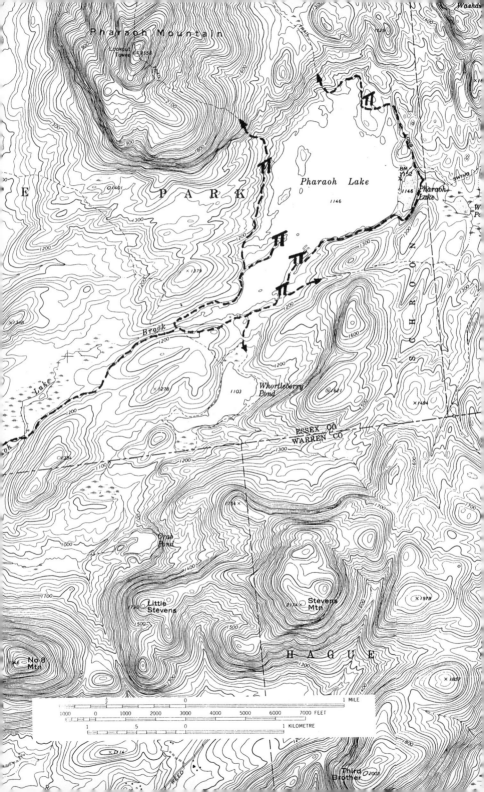

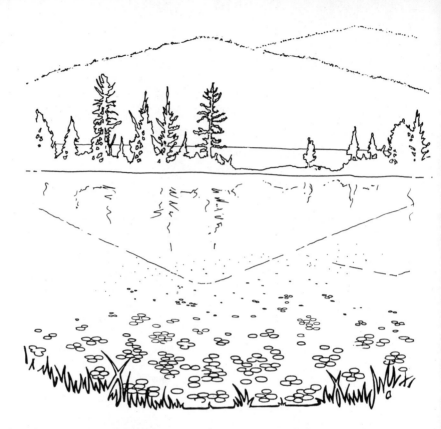

The trail to the lake follows an old road. After parking on Pharaoh Lake Road, walk north for 1 mile to Mill Creek and cross it on a plank bridge. The 100 yards of trail beyond the bridge is usually flooded. Hikers often have to take off their boots to wade through the water! The trail continues through a reforestation area (where trees have been planted). Numerous log roads turn out from the road/trail, which has few blue markers, but the main road is always obvious. At 2.15 miles there is a left fork to a good camping spot on an evergreen promontory above the meadows that surround Pharaoh Lake Brook.

The right fork, with both red and yellow markers, crosses the brook and follows the flow for a time. A good-sized beaver dam just above the bridge has turned these meadows into quite a pond. At 3.4 miles there is a marked intersection with the Sucker Brook Horse Trail and just beyond is a junction with the West Shore Trail. If you choose that trail, you pass a spring in 0.1 mile and at 0.4 mile pass a right fork to the first of the three lean-tos that sit on the west shore.

The trail forks again at 0.75 mile where a yellow-marked spur leads right for 0.3 mile to two lean-tos on a pine- and hemlock-covered promontory. It is 4.6 miles from the trailhead to these lean-tos.

The left fork, the red-marked West Shore Trail, continues to parallel the shore until 1.6 miles from the first approach to the lake, where it turns northwest for the steep climb up Pharaoh Mountain. It is easy to make this 1.6-mile, 1400-foot climb as a side trip while you are camping on the west shore.

If you chose to camp along the east shore, continue east from your first approach to the lake on the yellow trail. In 0.4 mile you pass campsites where there once were lean-tos, and just past them a side trail leads to Whortleberry Pond. The first lean-to is at 0.7 mile and just beyond it a fork right to Springhill Pond. At 0.9 mile you see a lean-to sitting on top of a long rock peninsula. The views of Pharaoh and Treadway mountains and the swimming area make this lean-to one of the best camping spots along the shore of Pharaoh Lake.

If you continue north, at 1.7 miles you reach a peninsula opposite Wintergreen Point. The trail to the point leads you for 0.8 mile around the north end of the lake. On the way you pass a right fork to Grizzle Ocean. If you walk around the north end of the lake, you reach a third lean-to not far from Split Rock Bay, one of the prettiest spots in the Adirondacks.

15 - Chub Pond

Distance - 3.7 miles to lean-to #2
Time - 2 hours
Trail markings - Blue foot-trail markers, orange snowmobile markers
Trailhead - From the flashing light on NY 28 at Woodgate, turn east onto Bear Creek Road and drive 3.2 miles to a parking area at the end of the road.
USGS map - McKeever

When you sit in front of the lean-to at the northern end of Chub Pond, you may notice the tops of the tallest trees swaying gently in the breeze. Sometimes great storms bring violent winds that bend even the strongest trees to the point where they break and fall. Often you see one or two large fallen trees along the trail, but near the outlet of Chub Pond, a great wind once toppled many trees all at once. This storm, which was probably a tornado, happened in 1984, and it will be many years before the woods here becomes tall and shady again.

From the trail register, Bear Creek Road becomes a rugged logging road. Walk along it for five minutes until you spot an older road with a yellow gate on your right. This is the way to Chub Pond. At 1.4 miles, a wooden bridge takes you across a large marshy area. This is the outlet of Gull Lake, which is described in the next section. About twenty minutes past this marsh you reach a junction where a yellow-marked trail heads north to that lake.

As you continue along the blue trail for another twenty-five minutes, you will notice a large bog through the trees to the right. Walk carefully to its edge and look for the many clumps of insectivorous pitcher plants--plants that can trap and consume insects.

In the distance on your right you can see the open water of Buck Pond. Here, the plants that are so special in a bog like this are close to the edge of the pond, and in some places grow on floating mats of sphagnum moss right out over its surface.

Back on the trail, you soon come to the edge of the Woodhull Creek Valley where the trail splits. There are two lean-tos at Chub Pond, which are connected by a trail. The right fork at this junction

leads toward the outlet of the pond and lean-to #1. The left fork leads down to lean-to #2, which has the prettiest location perched above a pebbly beach.

From lean-to #2, take the connecting trail southwest along the pond to its outlet where you will see the first of the fallen trees. Across the outlet you walk through the center of the blowdown, which is still very open. Here you will find a yellow-marked trail that passes lean-to #1 and continues on south to Stone Dam Pond. Amazingly, even though this lean-to is surrounded by fallen trees, it was not damaged by that storm. It now has a supply of firewood that will last for years!

16 - Gull Lake

Distance - 3.6 miles in, 4.6 miles out
Time - 2 to 2½ hours for each leg of the trip
Trail markings - Yellow, then red, then yellow foot trail markers, orange snowmobile markers
Trailhead - From the flashing light on NY 28 at Woodgate, turn east onto Bear Creek Road and drive 3.2 miles to a parking area at the road's official end.
USGS map - McKeever

Gull Lake has many tall, dead standing trees along its shore that were killed when beaver dams raised the water level, cutting oxygen off from the trees' roots. Eventually, when the beavers leave and their dams fall apart, the water level will drop and the skeletons of trees will stand for a time in a grassy meadow. Eventually they will fall and new trees will begin to grow in these places, which are often called beaver meadows. This cycle of tree growth is important for a healthy environment because it provides many different habitats for

the creatures of the woods. At Gull Lake, you can see how ospreys, smaller cousins of the eagle, have found an ideal nesting spot in the tops of these dead trees.

Start out from the Bear Creek Road trailhead as for Chub Pond, but this time, continue straight ahead on the logging road for about ten minutes to a second junction. Turn left here and hike down the yellow-marked trail into the Bear Creek Valley. Look for two old unmarked roads that branch off to your left. Either of these will take you quickly down to the creek where you may surprise deer, ducks, and maybe even a great blue heron.

After hiking for about 2 miles, you arrive at a junction where you will turn right onto a red-marked trail. Slowly but steadily you climb through the tall hardwood forest to the top of a small hill, crossing the logging road along the way. The red-marked trail ends at yet another junction with a yellow-marked trail. A left turn here will take you down to the lean-to at Gull Lake, 0.5 mile away. It is nestled among the trees on the north side of the lake, and if you walk along the shore to the right, you will find some large rocks where you can enjoy your lunch. Nearby are the tall trunks of dead trees, two of which are topped with osprey nests. If you arrive in the late spring or early summer, you may see a pair of ospreys diving into the water for fish to feed their hungry youngsters hidden in one of the nests.

You may hike out the way you came or make a loop by taking a different route. From the junction at the top of the hill, stay on the yellow trail, following it south and east around the lake. After crossing the lake's outlet, you arrive at a beautiful bay with many magnificent dead standing trees. Leaving the lake, you walk south through a deep, peaceful woods eventually coming to the blue-marked Chub Pond trail. Turn right at this junction for the rest of the easy hike out.

If you are prepared for an extra day of camping, you can turn left at this junction and visit Chub Pond as described in the previous section. This makes a marvelous three-day outing with two nights spent at different lean-tos and will give you an idea of what it is like to make even longer camping trips. If you do visit both lean-tos you will hike 3.6 miles the first day, 4.3 miles the second, and 3.7 miles the last day for a total of 11.6 miles.

17 - Middle Settlement Lake

> **Distance** - 3.6 miles one-way
> **Time** - 2 hours
> **Trail markings** - Yellow
> **Trailhead** - A section of old highway marked with DEC signs turns left from NY 28 2.9 miles north of the bridge at McKeever, rejoining NY 28 0.5 miles further, across from Singing Waters Campground. The trailhead is located near the midpoint, where a dirt road heads northwest.
> **USGS Map** - Thendara

With so many interesting things to discover, Middle Settlement Lake will become one of your favorite places to visit. There is a lean-to on the northwest shore, many additional places to pitch your tent, several rocks to swim from and picnic on, a nearby lookout, even an area of giant boulders with a cave. You are likely to see loons on the lake and hear ravens in the air; there may even be a new beaver colony.

Begin your trip by hiking up the dirt road to a gate. Not far beyond, a trail register on the left marks the beginning of a recently constructed foot trail. This section of trail goes through an easement, a portion of private land where the owner has given the public the rights to enter. Until recently, hikers used a different route to get to Middle Settlement Lake, so the foot tread here is not as well worn. Be sure to keep watching for the yellow markers to stay on course.

The new trail crosses the dirt road at 0.4 mile, then winds on to cross a small stream. Rising up and over a small hill it reaches the Copper Lake Road at 0.8 mile. Turning left, the trail follows the road for 0.4 mile, then turns right and enters the Ha-De-Ron-Dah Wilderness. This section of trail follows the route of one of the first roads into the area. It was known as the Brown's Tract Road and early settlers began using it over 150 years ago. Imagine, in half a mile you have gone from one of the newest trails in the Adirondacks to one of the oldest!

The trail drops to cross a small stream in a rocky glen, then climbs to a junction where the trail to Middle Settlement Lake forks left. In fifteen minutes you cross an attractive little vly or wet meadow, turning right on the other side. Rolling terrain takes you to a major

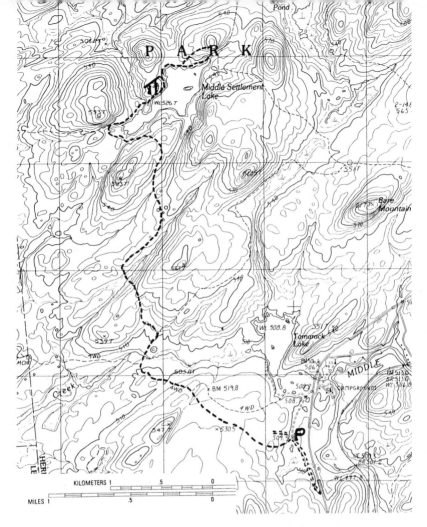

stream crossing in twenty minutes. Climbing easily over one more hill, the trail descends to a campsite on the southern end of the lake. From here, the trail swings left around the lake, passing the Lost Lake trail junction and crossing the outlet before reaching the lean-to.

Continuing north, then east, the trail nears the northern end of the lake where a red trail turns left, climbing 0.5 mile to a scenic lookout. Down below, the yellow trail enters a draw filled with giant boulders. At the base of some cliffs, one large slab rests on other rocks forming a cave. This makes a good shelter for hikers and animals alike! Trails continue on from this area but for those you will want a map and guidebook.

18 - Panther Pond

Distance - 4.4 miles one-way
Time - 2 1/2 hours
Trail markings - None along Smith Road, snowmobile markers and yellow trail markers along last section
Trailhead - A DEC sign marks the trailhead at the beginning of Smith Road, which is 1 mile west of the intersection with Buck Point Road in the settlement of Number Four; or 4.2 miles east of Crystal Lake Road. Four-wheel-drive vehicles can be driven 3.5 miles south on Smith Road to an interior parking area. All other vehicles can park near Number Four Road.
USGS Map - Number Four

The lean-to at Panther Pond is one of the most well-kept in the Adirondacks. Though it is not difficult to reach, it is in one of the park's most underused. Though it is possible to take a four-wheel-drive vehicle to within a mile of the pond, you will want to hike the whole distance to enjoy the many stream crossings, changing forest cover, and easy grades.

From Number Four Road, hike south along Smith Road, which is a wide dirt and gravel road. At several points along its 3.5-mile length, you will see turnouts, which are designated camping areas used mostly by hunters in the autumn. The road descends gradually to the valley of Burnt Creek, then parallels the creek before turning south to cross it. If you look closely in the dirt, you may see the tracks of raccoons, fishers, or otters who have crossed the road as they follow the creek looking for prey.

Smith Road officially ends at an interior parking area marked by a DEC sign. Swinging right, the road descends past a gate, then crosses Pine Creek. It is now designated as a snowmobile-and-foot trail and in just over 0.1 mile, it comes to a junction and register. The way left goes into the heart of the Independence River Wild Forest, connecting with many other trails and old roads. You will want a map or guidebook to explore them.

Sign in at the register and take the narrower trail on the right. It descends to the edge of wetlands along Pine Creek, and depending on beaver activity, it can be flooded in several spots. Carefully make your way along this stretch for 0.1 mile until the trail rises and

becomes drier. It then crests a hill and drops easily to Panther Pond and the lean-to.

The trail turns left at the lean-to, becoming a narrow foot trail that heads southwest to the Independence River. Not far from the lean-to, it passes a spring trickling into the pond. It is a good source for clear water, but like all water gathered in the wild, it should be purified.

19 - Wanika Falls

Distance - 6.8 miles one-way
Time - 3.5 hours
Trail markings - Blue
Trailhead - Drive 1.1 miles south on Averyville Road from the Old Military Road. The trailhead and parking area are located on the left, just before the bridge over the Chubb River.
USGS Map - Saranac Lake and Ampersand Lake

Try the backpack in to Wanika Falls after you have gained confidence on some of the easier trips in this book. The trail is popular and well-maintained, but over its length there are several ups and downs that can tire the inexperienced backpacker. Add to this a few tricky stream crossings and the occasional blowdown, and you've got a bit of a challenge. This is part of the true backpacking experience, however, and the beauty of Wanika Falls will reward your efforts.

From the parking area, the trail follows an old logging road past the register, then strikes off to the left and begins to rise away from the Chubb River. Over the next few miles, you will cross many streams that flow to the west. If the woods is wet, use caution on the logs and boards--they can be very slippery! Beaver flooding occasionally covers portions of the trail in these areas so watch for detours and return to the main trail as soon as possible.

The trail crosses the Chubb River near a series of waterfalls at 6.1 miles. Though you are getting close to the lean-to, you will want to stop and admire, maybe photograph, these falls. At 6.7 miles, the side trail to the lean-to branches left and crosses the river. In times of high water, this can be difficult so move cautiously and lend helping hands to others in your group. Wanika Falls is east of the lean-to, which is in disrepair and may be removed in the future.

From a campsite here, you can enjoy a day trip southwest to Moose Pond, which also has a lean-to. Imagine, you will have hiked the northernmost 9 miles of the famous 132-mile long Northville-Placid Trail. As you continue to gain more backpacking experience, you may find yourself getting anxious to do the rest of it!

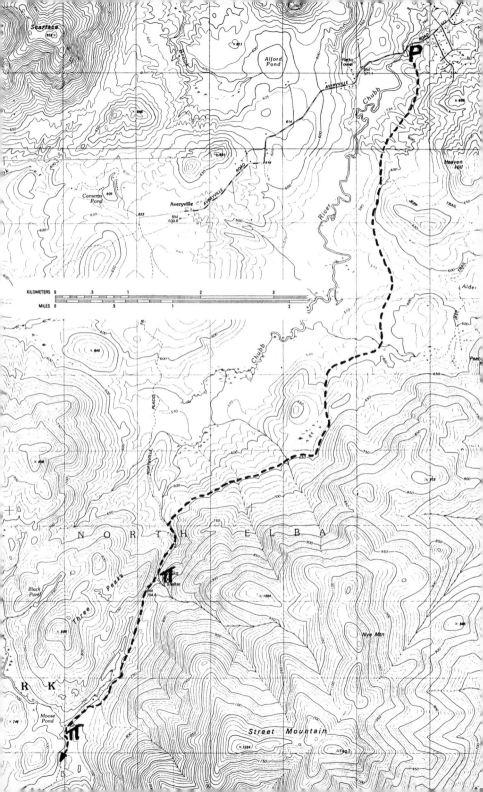

Destinations without lean-tos

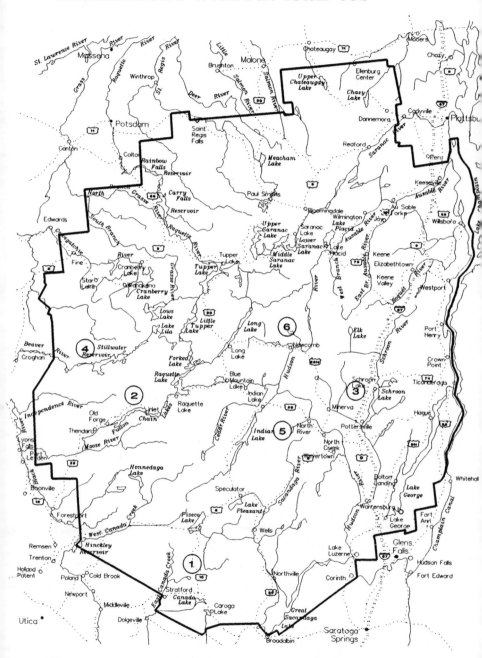

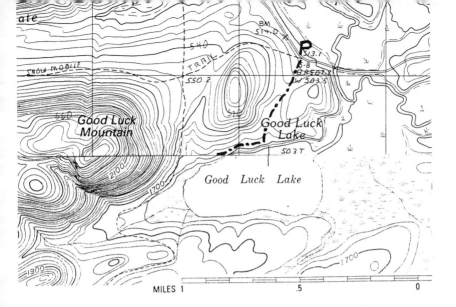

1 - Good Luck Lake

> **Distance** - 0.5 mile one-way
> **Time** - ½ hour
> **Trail markings** - None, this is an unmarked footpath
> **Trailhead** - The parking turnout is on the west side of NY 10, just north of the second bridge over the West Branch of the Sacandaga River in Arietta. The path begins across the road.
> **USGS Maps** - Canada Lake and Morehouse Mtn.

Good Luck Lake has such a short path that it is a good destination for a first backpack trip. It is also a popular camping destination because its northern shore, which slopes gently to the lake, has several nice, dry campsites with good swimming nearby.

Opposite the parking area, a marked snowmobile trail leads toward Dry and Dexter lakes and toward Spectacle Lake. Just to the right of the marked trail, a small path leads into the woods. It is not marked but it is easy to follow as it climbs a small knoll and descends to the lakeshore.

You can walk around the western shores of the lake, canoe to the lake to your campsite, walk along the trail toward Spectacle Lake, or, with the USGS maps and guidebook, you may want to try the bushwhack to Good Luck Cliffs.

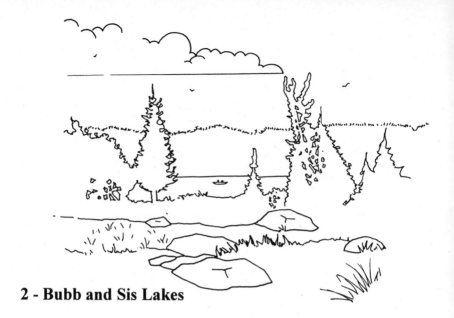

2 - Bubb and Sis Lakes

Distance - 2 miles one-way, slight rise
Time - 1 hour or so
Trail markings - Yellow markings
Trailhead - Opposite the Country Lane Gift Shop, which is on NY 28 1.5 miles southwest of Big Moose Road or 7.6 miles from the Old Forge information center. Note there is limited parking on the shoulder of the road.
USGS Map - Eagle Bay

In the early 1800s, Charles Herreshoff tried to open an iron mine and build a forge near Thendara. When the mine flooded, he shot himself in despair. Otis Arnold took over the mansion Herreshoff had built and raised a huge family. One of his sons, Ed, a guide, was said to have caught and eaten more fish than anyone else in the Adirondacks. Bubb was his favorite fishing lake and it is said that is how his nickname became the name of the lake. Sis Lake was named for one of his ten sisters, but which one is not known.

The trail to Bubb and Sis lakes is another very good beginner camping trip, short and easy, where you can practice backcountry camping skills in a lovely setting. These two pretty little lakes are separated by a narrow rise only 200 yards wide. Not only can you see both lakes from the rise, but it also offers a pleasant camping spot. There is also a nice campsite on the north shore of Bubb Lake,

84

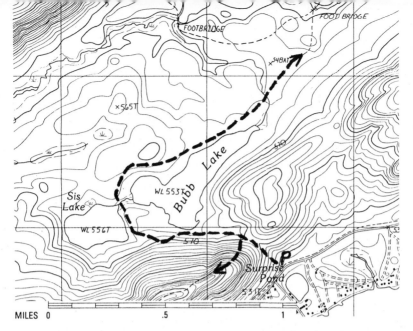

MILES 0   .5   1

though there is none on the south shore, your first approach to the
lake. Both lakes are good for picnicking, swimming, and boating if
you bring a canoe or inflatable boat. Best of all, the surrounding
forest has some magnificent spruce and hemlock trees as well as
hardwoods.

At the beginning of the trail, you climb uphill for five minutes to a
left fork to the blue-marked Vista Trail. If you have time, hide your
pack and climb to the first lookout to see Bubb Lake. Your route
straight ahead is still uphill, but quickly levels off. You follow a
small stream, then cross it, and after 0.5 mile come to a fork where
the trail turns left. A narrow path leads straight ahead at the fork to
the southern shore of Bubb Lake.

Continuing on the trail, you pass a small path also on your left that
leads to the south shore of Sis Lake. A second left fork is the better
route to the lake; it leads to a picnic site beneath tall hemlocks. The
trail turns northerly and in just a few yards passes a good campsite.
Just beyond you cross the outlet of Sis Lake; from here you can see
both lakes. After a short rise, the trail turns east to follow the northern
shore of Bubb Lake where you will find another campsite. The walk
along the north shore takes about twenty minutes. The trail turns
north at the northeast corner of the lake and continues on to Moss
Lake, where you will need a permit from a DEC ranger to camp.

3 - Big Pond

Distance - 1.6 miles one-way
Time - 1 hour
Trail markings - Blue
Trailhead - A small parking area on the north side of Hoffman Road, 2.1 miles west of Schroon Lake village. There is additional parking along the road nearby. The trail begins along an old road closed to vehicles by three small boulders.
USGS Map - Schroon Lake

Big Pond is on the southern border of the Hoffman Notch Wilderness Area. It is a beautiful little pond with several campsites around its drier shores. You may see wildlife--kingfishers and hawks, muskrats and beavers--both on the way and while you are at the pond. There is an extensive marsh along the southwestern inlet of the pond. Walking along the pond's shore will take you to a very beautiful hemlock knoll as well as close enough to the wetlands to see many birds.

The trail climbs very gradually, and during a ten-minute walk from the trailhead it drops gently to a sturdy wooden bridge, which is just downstream from a six-foot-tall beaver dam. The dam, across Big Pond's outlet brook, holds back a sizable beaver pond. Just beyond the bridge you can spot stumps that beavers have chewed. In another five minutes look for the unmarked path to North Pond to your right. If you notice three large clumps of cedar trees on your left and a clump of birches on your right, you should spot the junction. Just beyond it, on the left, there is a large white pine with a double trunk.

Continuing on the blue trail for another twenty minutes, you climb a couple of gentle grades and then spot a large erratic (a boulder dropped by a receding glacier) about 40 feet to the left of the trail. Here the trail becomes narrower and winds downhill for less than five minutes. As the trail begins to level off, at about 1.5 miles, it makes a sharp right turn. At this point an unmarked path heads left through a depression then up onto a low ridge. Walk straight along this ridge, with a wetland below on your right. In just a few minutes you are on

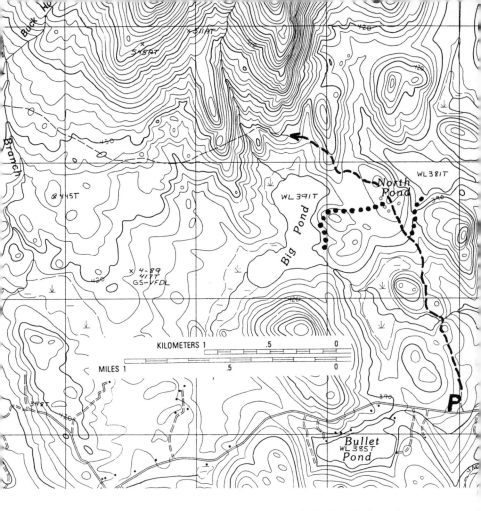

a hemlock-covered promontory at the edge of Big Pond. It makes a lovely campsite.

The blue trail continues around the north end of the pond if you want to explore further. With a map and compass there are several other things to do while you are camping at the pond. The old road that takes you to the pond continues west beyond the pond for 1.8 miles to a crossing of the East Branch of Trout Brook where there is a very beautiful picnic spot. You can walk north following the brook to look for waterfalls. Alternatively, you can branch from the old road that leads to the pond and find the short path that leads to North Pond. From here you can enjoy the bushwhack to the slopes of Jones Hill. (For this you should have the USGS map or a guidebook.)

4 - Jakes Pond

Distance - 4.1 miles one-way
Time - 2½ to 3 hours
Trail markings - Red
Trailhead - Park just before the gate on Long Pond Road, at the clearing known as Bergren's for the old sportsmen's hotel which was located here. Take Belfort Road northeast from NY 812 at Croghan, cross the Beaver River in Belfort, and at a T just beyond, turn right onto Long Pond Road. This continues northeast for 10.3 miles to Bergren's. The trailhead is down an old roadway on the southwest side of the clearing.
USGS Map - Stillwater

Walk the trail to Jakes Pond to enjoy the wildlife you will see on the way. The Jakes Pond trail takes you past some very pretty waterways, through forested ridges, and along a number of beaver meadows. It is possible that one or more of the meadows will have active beaver dams, flooding the trail. This has happened repeatedly over the years, so it is possible you may never reach Jakes Pond. No matter--you can find several nice campsites along the trail and many places to explore. The pond is on the western edge of a large tract of land known as Watson's East Triangle, much of which was acquired by the state from a logging company in 1986.

The trail begins on private land and continues for 1.6 miles on easement land. The easement gives the public permission to walk the trail, but no camping is allowed. From the trailhead, the trail descends to cross the West Branch of the Oswegatchie River on a bridge that is near a waterfall. At 1 mile, the trail crosses the river again, then you see the first of many beaver flows. At 1.6 miles signs indicate you have entered state land where camping is permitted. Ridges of evergreens border wetlands and marshes. At 2 miles the old Keck Trail forks left. You take the right fork and at 2.2 miles cross the West Branch for a third time. You may want to camp nearby or look for another spot farther on.

At 2.5 miles you reach a large beaver meadow; corduroy (logs placed across the trail) helps you through a wetland at 2.8 miles. You can find a level spot to camp in the next stretch, but it may be buggy. The trail has been detoured across a beaver dam so it can continue

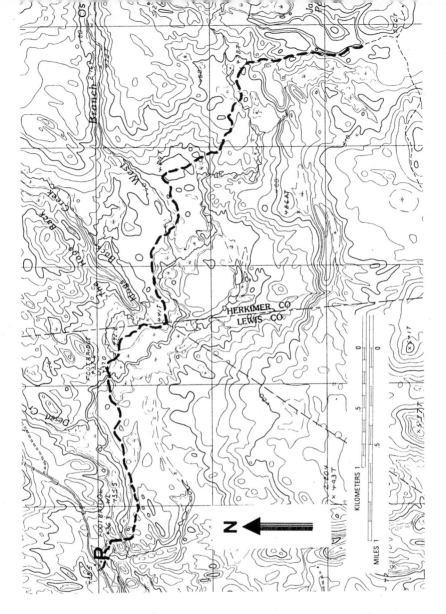

around another wetland at 3.2 miles. A new trail has been cut through a fringe of forest. Beyond is a new beaver pond that floods the trail. If it has dried out, you can continue across it and then over a small hill for the last stretch of trail, 0.9 mile, down to Jakes Pond. The pond is long and thin, clasped between two steep ridges that are topped with tall evergreens, so it's not the easiest place to find a flat camping spot.

5 - Hour Pond

Distance - 4.4 miles one-way
Time - 3 hours
Trail markings - Blue markings, part way, unmarked path the rest.
Trailhead - Thirteenth Lake Road heads south of North River for 3.5 miles to a fork. Right leads to Thirteenth Lake boat launch; you go left. Stay straight on Old Farm Road where the road to Garnet Hill Lodge turns left, uphill. In 0.75 mile you reach the new trailhead for the east side of Thirteenth Lake.
USGS Map - Thirteenth Lake

Hour Pond nestles among bulky mountains in the northwest part of the Siamese Ponds Wilderness Area. Its remote location and the fact that you are not apt to see other campers make it a wonderful wilderness destination. Because part of the approach is along an unmarked path it is also a challenging trek.

Old Farm Road, now closed to vehicles, continues south from the trailhead, out of sight of Thirteenth Lake. It leads in 1.2 miles to Old Farm Clearing, a reforestation area, where you will find a registration box. Be sure to sign in. Continue walking south on the roadway for 200 yards to a right fork to the west. It is marked with blue, but so is the continuing old road, which you should not follow.

At 2.5 miles, 1.3 miles from Old Farm Clearing, the trail crosses a stream that drains Buck Meadow Flow. Beyond the bridge, the trail climbs and begins to follow the outlet of Hour Pond. That stream has a lovely series of small waterfalls and a miniature flume, where there's a good place to stop and rest.

Just beyond the top of the falls, the trail crosses Hour Pond Outlet on a log bridge. Then in a hundred yards or so, the blue trail, which continues on to Puffer Pond, crosses the stream again. Before you reach this second crossing, which is 3 miles from the beginning, look to your right and you will discover the beginning of an unmarked path that leads gently uphill. With several diversions, the path generally follows the outlet of Hour Pond to the pond.

At first the path is high on a ridge above the outlet. After about twenty minutes, the path descends and curves around the head of a small draw. Turning back and descending some more, the path

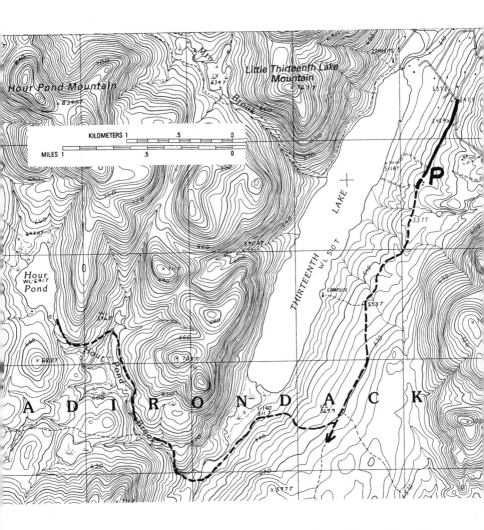

reaches a campsite near a dried-up beaver meadow. The old dam that
created the beaver flow serves as a path across the wet area. This is a
very pretty spot. At the end, turn sharply left to follow the border of
the marshes. The path has turned almost south to go around the side
of a steep hill. If you have trouble following the path, remember to let
one of your party stay on a visible part of the path while you look
about for the continuing route.

The path turns back north, climbs beside a small draw and reaches
another beaver meadow. Beyond the meadow the path is close to the

outlet stream, then it veers away from it to climb over a small rise and descend to the shore of the pond. You can find several flat places to camp, but be sure to choose one 150 feet back from the pond. The view across the pond is of the cliffs on Hour Pond Mountain and to the south to Bullhead Mountain.

With the USGS map or a guidebook, you can continue west from the Hour Pond Outlet bridge on the eastern trail to Puffer Pond or even on to John Pond for a long backpack trip of at least three nights.

6 - Moose Pond

> **Distance** - 7 miles one-way
> **Time** - 3½ to 4 hours
> **Trail Markings** - Blue horse trail markers
> **Trailhead** - Santanoni Preserve trailhead in Newcomb, just north of NY 28 N.
> **USGS Maps** - Newcomb and Santanoni Peak

The length of the trail to Moose Pond makes this a difficult walk with a pack, so consider Moose Pond a challenge to see if you are ready for longer backpack trips. The pond has good campsites and swimming. The access trail continues north to cross Ermine Brook, Callahan Brook, and Moose Creek. If you get this far on a day hike from your campsite, you might want to continue north to Shattuck Clearing on the Cold River. For this you should have the USGS map and a guidebook.

Moose Pond lies southwest of Santanoni Peak. The old roadway that gives access to the pond is often used by groups of campers on horseback. They tend to cluster at the southern end of the pond, in the fields back from the shore of the lake where there is a good campsite. You can find other good campsites along the east shore. If you walk through the fields to the shore of the pond, there is a great view of the Ermine Brook slide--a long white gash on the slopes of Santanoni where trees, rocks, and boulders were torn from the mountainside in a heavy rain a few years ago.

From the parking area for Newcomb Lake, walk north for 2.2 miles to a fork and turn left. The trail winds along on high ground for almost a mile, to a bridge with a campsite nearby. Beyond a second bridge at 3.3 miles, the trail climbs to a height-of-land, then begins a long gentle downhill. At 4.3 miles the trail emerges from forest into open fields, some bordered with long wetlands. There are great views here of the Ermine Brook Slide. At 5.9 miles the trail begins to climb into the col between Moose Mountain and an unnamed mountain. Near the height-of-land in the col, the blue horse trail splits. The left fork heads downhill to the south shore of Moose Pond.

If you have enjoyed these camping destinations, you may want to try some others.

Other camping destinations

There are hundreds more great camping destinations in the Adirondack Park than the twenty-five camping trips described in this introductory guide. Here are some hints on how to use other basic hiking or trail guides to expand your opportunities. You may already have these guides, listed below, or you can find them in the library. A few of the suggested trails go to lean-tos, and one is at the end of a canoe trip. Most are moderately long trails and four involve some elevation change, making them more challenging for backpackers than the ones in this guide. In addition, there are other day hikes in these guides that can be combined to make good camping trips.

Each hike in these guides has a map that will show you the route of the trail. Hikes 1 through 5 are from *Adventures in Hiking*. Hikes 6 and 7 are from *Fun on Flatwater*, and Hikes 8 through 14 are from *50 Hikes in the Adirondacks*.

1 - Grassy and Wilson Pond

These two ponds are south of Blue Mountain Lake. Wilson Pond is on the shoulder of Blue Ridge, the mountain that gives its name to the surrounding wilderness area. The lean-to on Wilson Pond is at the end of the 2.9-mile long trail. It is sited on a beautiful point facing the Blue Ridge Mountains. You climb more than 300 feet to the pond, so allow 2½ to 3 hours with a pack.

2 - Peaked Mountain Pond

Peaked Mountain is south of North River and its trailhead is the boat launch for Garnet Lake. The trail to Peaked Mountain is one of the most challenging. The walk to the pond for camping on the way to the mountain is also quite challenging. Be sure you have a copy of the hiking guide and a map if you plan to camp here. If you plan to hike to the mountaintop from your campsite you will definitely need a good trail guide. The trail from the parking area at Thirteenth Lake to the pond is 2.5 miles long, fairly strenuous because it rises 570 feet, and occasionally difficult because it has few markings. With a pack allow as much as three hours for the walk to the pond. There are several campsites along both north and south shores, but be sure to find one that is at least 150 feet from water. (Most of the campsites others have used are too close to water.)

3 - Rock and Long Ponds

The guide describes a 3.5-mile trail whose trailhead is at the end of a very long and very rough dirt road through private lands. The road heads north from Speculator and just getting to the trailhead is an adventure, but the trail is relatively level and easy, making it great for backpacking. There is a wonderful camping spot at Rock Pond 2.6 miles from the trailhead on a bank above the pond where there is good swimming. You may want to camp here and visit Long Pond on a day hike during your stay. If you do go to Long Pond to camp, note that the wonderful long thin peninsula that juts from the west shore of the pond is too close to the water to be considered a campsite, even though others have camped there.

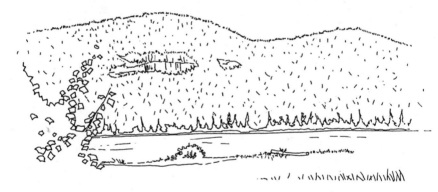

4 - Tirrell Pond

Tirrell Pond is also near Blue Mountain Lake and one trail to the pond starts from the same parking area as the trail up Blue Mountain. Tirrell Pond has two lean-tos, the first being near its north end at the end of a 3.25-mile trail. You descend 500 feet from the trailhead to the pond, so the hard part of the backpacking will come at the end of your stay. While you are at the pond, you will find a good trail along the south shore. It leads in 1.1 miles to a second lean-to, this one very close to the outlet of the pond. There is a path of sorts around the north shore and you will find several places with sandy beaches and good swimming. The fishing is good and you should see otters and loons. If you can arrange a drop-off, you can walk out via the trail that leads from the eastern end of the pond to the trailhead opposite Lake Durant.

5 - Mitchell Ponds

A road that begins west of Indian Lake and follows the Cedar River continues as a dirt track through the Moose River Recreation Area to a T, where it turns back north past Limekiln Lake to Inlet. The trail to Mitchell Ponds starts just north of the T. There is no lean-to at Mitchell Ponds, but there is a nice campsite at the end of the 2-mile, relatively level trail. There are flat patches on the south shore for camping and a path along the north shore so you can see the interesting plants and ferns and views that make this such a lovely spot.

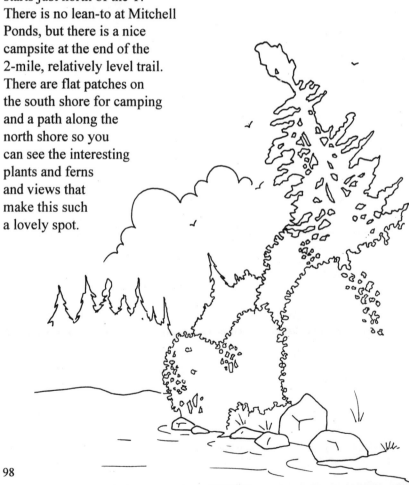

6 - Lixard Pond

One Lixard Pond trailhead is accessible by water, the other by a difficult dirt road and a long trail. Lixard Pond is a wonderful, long, thin pond with hemlock-covered shores nestled beneath Mount Blue, plus there is a nice lean-to, so those are worth the difficulties of getting there. The canoe guide tells where to launch a canoe on Garnet Lake, which is south of Johnsburg. Paddle across the lake in a south-southwesterly direction. On the south shore near the entrance to Garnet Lake's southeastern lobe, a sign on shore designates the trailhead. Snowmobile markers designate the trail that leads almost a mile southwest to Lixard Pond then follows the shore more than 0.5 mile to the lean-to, which is near the pond's western end.

7 - Newcomb Lake

The canoe guide tells you about hiring a horse and wagon to take you and your canoe in to Newcomb Lake. The access road, where only maintenance vehicles are permitted, is a broad, easy-to-walk roadway. Although the distance to the lake is over 6 miles and it is even farther to the best campsites, the swimming and exploring are great enough to encourage you to camp either along the south shore, where there is a lean-to, or on the north shore beyond the lodge, where there are wonderful swimming beaches.

8 - Murphy, Middle and Bennett Lakes

These lakes form a chain that is east of NY 30 near Hope, north of Northville. The lean-to on Murphy Lake is halfway between the two trailheads that connect this 7.2-mile trail. You can visit it on a walk through if you can arrange a drop off and pick up, or you can walk to it from either end and explore the other ponds while you are camping at the lean-to. All three are lovely little lakes with nice swimming spots and other good places to camp if the lean-to is full. Middle Lake has an island, the best primitive campsites, and a path of sorts around the eastern shore that leads to other high and dry campsites.

9 - Cascade and Stephens Ponds

These ponds are southwest of Blue Mountain Lake. There are two lean-tos on the 7.5-mile loop described that visits both ponds. One part of the loop is along the Northville-Placid Trail that passes through Lake Durant Campground. The other trailhead is near the north end of Lake Durant, just off NY 30. There is enough elevation change that you may want to plan a two-night trip visiting both lean-tos. If not, I prefer the lean-to at Stephens Pond, where there is good trout fishing in early spring. You are sure to see loons and other wildlife.

10 - Queer Lake

Queer Lake is in the Pigeon Lake Wilderness south of Big Moose Lake. The shortest of the two approaches to Queer Lake is less than 3 miles and continues around the north side of the lake to a long, thin peninsula with a lean-to. The evergreen-covered shores of this deep wilderness lake do not invite walking around, but there are several additional trails in the vicinity leading to other lakes and ponds with campsites or to more new places to explore.

11 - Gleasmans Falls

Gleasmans Falls is in the Independence River Wild Forest in the far western Adirondacks. The 3-mile trail to the falls is a fairly easy backpack trip. There is no lean-to, but there are several camping spots. When you walk along the gorge beside the falls, be very careful. You can find good, level camping places before you reach the gorge. The trail continues past the gorge and you may want to continue along it on a dayhike from your campsite.

12 - East Branch of the Sacandaga River and Siamese Ponds

There are no lean-tos on the Siamese Ponds but that does not deter fishermen and campers. The trailhead parking lot off NY 8 west of Johnsburg often has many cars. If you camp at the lean-to on the East Branch of the Sacandaga for two nights, you can make a day-trip excursion to explore both ponds. Beginning backpackers may want to camp at the lean-to on the river, since it is a 3.9-mile walk one way, and the return over the shoulder of Eleventh Mountain is a steep climb with a pack. The round trip to the ponds adds 5.4 miles and that, too, has some uphill sections. If you plan to camp at the ponds, be sure you are up to the 13.2-mile round trip.

13 - T Lake

It is quite a walk to the T Lake lean-to if you are carrying a pack. The one-way distance is 4 miles but the elevation change is nearly 1,000 feet. This trek will give you experience for carrying a backpack in mountainous regions. The trail, in the southern part of the West Canada Lakes Wilderness Area, starts at Poplar Point Campground on Piseco Lake. The lake is shaped like an inverted T, with its long, thin, bony arms stretching along the trail. There are other good campsites along the lake's southern shore.

14 - Lake Lila

Lake Lila is west of NY 30 and south of Tupper Lake. The walk to the former site of William Seward Webb's Nehasane Lodge takes you around the north shore of Lake Lila. Open fields make good camping destinations. A side trip up Frederica Mountain is a wonderful addition to any trip to this area. The walk is not nearly as much fun as the trip by canoe to a campsite on the western shore or on one of the islands.

Putting together a long backpacking trip

After you have made several overnight or weekend camping trips, you may want to put together a longer trip, perhaps as long as five or six days. For this kind of a trip, you will need a more detailed guidebook, such as one of the *Discover* Series. Because you have to be self-sufficient for that long, your planning will be more complicated. Study the USGS maps carefully and plan your trip with segments that are manageable and places to stop that are interesting. Make sure you note all the intersections and have a plan to shorten your trip if something does go wrong. Be sure not only that you tell someone where you are going, but leave an itinerary that lists your planned campsites and the routes you might take if you have to shorten your trip.

On a two-day trip you can often avoid rain by postponing your trip if rain is forecasted; on a six-day trip in the Adirondacks you will almost certainly have rain. You may want an extra change of clothes, certainly an extra pair of socks beyond the two you normally have. Be sure you have moleskin and antibiotic ointment—you will be fortunate indeed if you don't get blisters.

Carrying enough food for five or six days is a challenge. After a few trips, you will know what you like and how much you need for each day of hiking. Plan not only for the amount you need, but plan for variety. What bothers me the most about carrying freeze-dried food and other mixes is that they are soft and mushy, and I get very tired of mush. Make sure you have enough things to munch and crunch on in your pack—crackers, granola bars, nuts and so on.

Be sure that you have a water filter that will last the whole time. When you plan your trip, the route you choose should take you near water every night, and the segments between water should be short enough to manage. Note the places where you can stop and filter water every couple of hours. When you do stop for a drink and filter water, fill your canteen, just in case. This is especially important in warm weather.

The following are just hints at the best long trips but those listed are my favorites—all are taken from the *Discover* Series. Pick one from an area where you enjoyed a camping trip described in this guide.

1 - The West Canada Lakes Wilderness Loop
(West Central Region)

Starting at Sled Harbor, which is northwest of Speculator, walk a loop that includes Pillsbury Lake, Whitney Lake, Sampson Lake, South Lake, and Big West. Add a day's detour to Brooktrout Lake and then go back to Big West. Continue on to the Cedar Lakes, stopping at both the south and north ends of the lake, and back out to Sled Harbor. This loop covers almost 30 miles and there are several ways to extend the trip. There are lean-tos all along the way and enough to see to extend the trip to six days and five nights.

2 - The Western High Peaks
(High Peaks Region)

There are several beginning and ending places for loops in the western High Peaks. If you can arrange it, plan a trip that starts and finishes at different trailheads. No matter which loop you choose, make sure you include the walk along the north shore of the Cold River on the Northville-Placid Trail, one of the most beautiful trails in the Adirondacks.

One loop starts along the Northville-Placid Trail from Long Lake to Shattuck Clearing, continues west to Duck Hole, fords the Cold River at the horse trail crossing west of Duck Hole, then heads back to Moose Pond and out to Santanoni trailhead. With detours to explore the surroundings, such as Blueberry Mountain or Pine Point on the Cold River, this can be a six-day, five-night trip.

A second route starts along the Northville-Placid Trail at Long Lake as far as Duck Hole, then continues on the Northville-Placid Trail north to Moose Pond and Wanika Falls. It ends at the end of the trail at Averyville, just south of Lake Placid.

For a third loop, walk as far as Duck Hole on the Northville-Placid Trail, then turn south over the shoulder of Santanoni Peak and out to the trailhead south of Tahawus. There is a big climb in this trip over the shoulder of Santanoni, especially with a pack.

3 - The Pharaoh Lake Wilderness
(Eastern Adirondacks Region)

Loops that exceed 20 miles and take four or five days can be started at several points in this wilderness area, which is east of the Northway near Schroon Lake. Detours to two mountains with trails and several without trails will extend the trip by a day or two. Plan your loop starting either at Crane Pond, Putnam Pond Campground, or Pharaoh Lake Trailhead. On the shortest trip, from Crane Pond trailhead, you can visit sixteen ponds in a 15-mile loop.

4 - The Silver Lake Wilderness Area
(Southern Adirondacks Region)

This wilderness is in the southern Adirondacks, west of NY 30 and northwest of Northville. No trail network forms a loop in the Silver Lake Wilderness Area, so the best long trip is a traverse along a segment of the Northville-Placid Trail. From the trailhead in Upper Benson, head west, then north for a stop at the Silver Lake lean-to. Continue north to stop at the Mud Lake lean-to, then continue on to the crossing of the West Branch of the Sacandaga River. From here, head northwest to the crossing of Hamilton Lake Stream. There is a lean-to just beyond. The trail continues to pass Priests Vly and marshes near Buckhorn Lake outlet before emerging along NY 8 near the school at Piseco. This trek is just over 22 miles long and is best divided into four days, with three nights camping at or near the lean-tos.

5 - The Five Ponds Wilderness Area
(Northwestern Adirondacks Region)

This wilderness area is in the northwestern region of the Adirondack Park, south of Cranberry Lake. The blowdown of July 1995 caused the greatest damage in the Five Ponds Wilderness Area, destroying forests in a broad swath from the northwest part of that area all the way southeast to Lake Lila. The network of trails offered several really good camping loops for trips of more than three days, but none are currently recommended until all the work is completed to reopen blocked trails.

6 - Ha-de-ron-dah Wilderness
(West Central Region)

The Ha-de-ron-dah Wilderness contains a fine network of trails offering many options for loop hikes or through trips. From Middle Settlement Lake you can continue east and north to Middle Branch Lake, then backtrack south and east around Cedar Pond, reaching the Brown Tract Trail for your westerly return to Copper Lake Road. For a longer and more adventurous loop, continue north from Middle Branch Lake to the Big Otter Trail. Turn left to visit Big Otter Lake, East Pine Pond, Pine Lake, and Lost Lake, finishing back at Middle Settlement Lake. This wonderful loop can be complicated by beaver flooding, so you may wish instead to turn right at the Big Otter Trail for a through hike to a second vehicle parked near Thendara.

7 - Black River Wild Forest
(Southwestern Adirondacks)

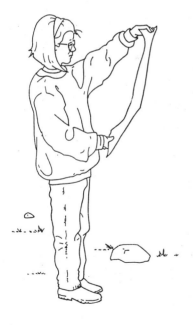

The Black River Wild Forest in the southwestern Adirondacks has a network of trails leading to ponds and waterfalls. Sections 15 and 16 describe routes that can be combined, but you can plan an even longer loop starting at the same Bear Creek Road trailhead by adding hikes to Woodhull Lake, Remsen Falls on the South Branch of the Moose, and Bear Lake. Such a trip could end either back at the Bear Creek Road trailhead or at the McKeever trailhead to the north if you can arrange to have a second vehicle parked there. This trip could easily be extended to four nights of camping.

Glossary

Adirondack Park - The lands in northern New York State within the Blue Line boundary first drawn in 1892 and enlarged in later years. The Adirondack Park contains both public and private lands.

Adirondack Park State Land Master Plan - A plan adopted by the Adirondack Park Agency and approved by the Governor of New York that directs the management of the Forest Preserve in the Adirondacks. The plan divides the Adirondacks into land classifications that receive different levels of protection. They are Wilderness, Wild Forest, Intensive Use, Canoe and Primitive areas.

Department of Environmental Conservation, or DEC - The state government department responsible for the care and management of the state's public lands, water and air.

Easement land - Private land whose owner has granted certain rights to the state. In some cases, those rights include public access. There may be restrictions against camping, fires or hunting.

Forest Preserve - The public lands within both the Adirondack and Catskill state parks. Forest Preserve lands are open to all people.

Forest Rangers - These DEC personnel are responsible for trail maintenance, issue camping permits, and perform rescues when necessary in the region of the state where they are assigned. Local rangers are listed in local phone books under New York State Department of Conservation. They can help if you need special information on conditions or trails in an area.

Guideboard - A sign at a trailhead designating the trail's destination, distances along the trail, and sometimes the elevation change along the trail's route.

Private land or posted land - Land that is not open to the public except by permission.

Trail Register - A box located near the beginning of a trail containing a notebook where all hikers and campers should sign in and out. Signing in is a safety measure that will help rescuers find you in an emergency.

Wilderness Area - Most wilderness areas are 10,000 acres or larger and they are protected so that they remain as natural as possible. No motorized vehicles are allowed; few structures except lean-tos and bridges are permitted in wilderness areas. They are places where you can enjoy solitude.

Wild Forest Area - An area which differs from a wilderness area in minor ways: snowmobiles are permitted in winter; mountain bikes are permitted on some trails; the areas are smaller; and they often have gravel-surface town roads leading into them.

Barbara McMartin is author or coauthor of twenty books about the Adirondacks. She has served on the Forest Preserve Advisory Committee and many other committees dealing with recreational planning and management of the Adirondack Forest Preserve. With her husband, she resides and works at Canada Lake, where she swims and walks with her grandchildren who have inspired her guides for young people.

Lee M. Brenning has coauthored four of McMartin's *Discover the Adirondacks* guides and has helped with revisions of other guides in that series. He and his wife, Georgie, are active outdoors people with careers just outside the park. They live in the Adirondacks near Nobleboro, on West Canada Creek.

Scott D. Selden holds a Bachelor of Fine Arts Degree from SUNY Fredonia and was a 1994 participant in the Yale University summer program in graphic design in Brissago, Switzerland. He is employed as a graphic designer and production manager at The Paige Smith Group in Utica, New York, where he also resides.

Other Books by Barbara McMartin

Books from North Country Books

Hides, Hemlocks and Adirondack History
The Great Forest of the Adirondacks
Adventures in Hiking,
    A Young Peoples' Guide to the Adirondacks
Fun on Flatwater,
    An Introduction to Adirondack Canoeing

Books from Lake View Publications

Discover the Adirondacks Series, written with
various co-authors

Discover the Adirondack High Peaks
Discover the Central Adirondacks
Discover the Eastern Adirondacks
Discover the Northeastern Adirondacks
Discover the Northern Adirondacks
Discover the South Central Adirondacks
Discover the Southeastern Adirondacks
Discover the Southern Adirondacks
Discover the Southwestern Adirondacks
Discover the West Central Adirondacks

Books from W. W. Norton

Fifty Hikes in the Adirondacks, Second Edition

All McMartin's books are distributed by
NORTH COUNTRY BOOKS
311 Turner Street
Utica, New York 13501
315-735-4877